D0582161

# In Green Pastures

# IN GREEN PASTURES

**Psalms** *for Everyday Life*

NEW INTERNATIONAL VERSION

Hodder & Stoughton
LONDON SYDNEY AUCKLAND

# SUBJECT INDEX

## SUBJECT INDEX

# SUBJECT INDEX

These are some selected references. The complete Bible contains many others relative to all the topics mentioned and more.

# PSALMS

## BOOK I (Psalms 1–41)

### Psalm 1

Blessed is the man
　　who does not walk in the
　　　　counsel of the wicked
or stand in the way of sinners
　　or sit in the seat of mockers.
But his delight is in the law of the
　　LORD,
　　and on his law he meditates
　　　　day and night.
He is like a tree planted by
　　　　streams of water,
　　which yields its fruit in season
and whose leaf does not wither.
　　Whatever he does prospers.

Not so the wicked!
　　They are like chaff
　　that the wind blows away.
Therefore the wicked will not
　　　　stand in the judgment,
　　nor sinners in the assembly of
　　　　the righteous.

For the LORD watches over the
　　　　way of the righteous,
　　but the way of the wicked will
　　　　perish.

### Psalm 2

Why do the nations conspire
　　and the peoples plot in vain?
The kings of the earth take their
　　　　stand
　　and the rulers gather together
　　　　against the LORD
　　and against his Anointed One.
"Let us break their chains," they
　　　　say,
　　"and throw off their fetters."

The One enthroned in heaven
　　　　laughs;
　　the Lord scoffs at them.
Then he rebukes them in his anger
　　and terrifies them in his wrath,
　　　　saying,
"I have installed my King
　　on Zion, my holy hill."

I will proclaim the decree of the
　　LORD:

He said to me, "You are my Son;
　　today I have become your
　　　　Father.
Ask of me,
　　and I will make the nations
　　　　your inheritance,

the ends of the earth your
    possession.
You will rule them with an iron
    sceptre;
    you will dash them to pieces
      like pottery."

Therefore, you kings, be wise;
    be warned, you rulers of the
      earth.
Serve the LORD with fear
    and rejoice with trembling.
Kiss the Son, lest he be angry
    and you be destroyed in your
      way,
for his wrath can flare up in a
    moment.
    Blessed are all who take refuge
    in him.

≈

## Psalm 3
*A psalm of David. When he fled from
his son Absalom.*

O LORD, how many are my foes!
    How many rise up against me!
Many are saying of me,
    "God will not deliver him."
                  *Selah*

But you are a shield around me,
    O LORD;
    you bestow glory on me and
    lift up my head.
To the LORD I cry aloud,
    and he answers me from his
      holy hill.      *Selah*

I lie down and sleep;
    I wake again, because the LORD
      sustains me.
I will not fear the tens of
    thousands
    drawn up against me on every
      side.

Arise, O LORD!
    Deliver me, O my God!
Strike all my enemies on the jaw;
    break the teeth of the wicked.

From the LORD comes deliverance.
    May your blessing be on your
      people.      *Selah*

≈

## Psalm 4
*For the director of music. With stringed
instruments. A psalm of David.*

Answer me when I call to you,
    O my righteous God.
Give me relief from my distress;
    be merciful to me and hear my
      prayer.

How long, O men, will you turn
    my glory into shame?
    How long will you love
      delusions and seek false
      gods?      *Selah*
Know that the LORD has set apart
    the godly for himself;
    the LORD will hear when I call
      to him.

In your anger do not sin;
    when you are on your beds,

search your hearts and be
  silent.                      *Selah*
Offer right sacrifices
  and trust in the LORD.

Many are asking, "Who can show
    us any good?"
  Let the light of your face shine
    upon us, O LORD.
You have filled my heart with
    greater joy
  than when their grain and new
    wine abound.
I will lie down and sleep in peace,
  for you alone, O LORD,
  make me dwell in safety.

~

## Psalm 5
*For the director of music. For flutes. A
psalm of David.*

Give ear to my words, O LORD,
  consider my sighing.
Listen to my cry for help,
  my King and my God,
  for to you I pray.
In the morning, O LORD, you hear
    my voice;
  in the morning I lay my
    requests before you
  and wait in expectation.

You are not a God who takes
    pleasure in evil;
  with you the wicked cannot
    dwell.
The arrogant cannot stand in your
    presence;

you hate all who do wrong.
You destroy those who tell lies;
  bloodthirsty and deceitful men
  the LORD abhors.

But I, by your great mercy,
  will come into your house;
in reverence will I bow down
  towards your holy temple.
Lead me, O LORD, in your
    righteousness
  because of my enemies—
  make straight your way before
    me.

Not a word from their mouth can
    be trusted;
  their heart is filled with
    destruction.
Their throat is an open grave;
  with their tongue they speak
    deceit.
Declare them guilty, O God!
  Let their intrigues be their
    downfall.
Banish them for their many sins,
  for they have rebelled against
    you.

But let all who take refuge in you
    be glad;
  let them ever sing for joy.
Spread your protection over
    them,
  that those who love your name
    may rejoice in you.
For surely, O LORD, you bless the
    righteous;
  you surround them with your
    favour as with a shield.

# Psalm 6

*For the director of music. With stringed instruments. According to* sheminith. *A psalm of David.*

O Lord, do not rebuke me in your
    anger
  or discipline me in your wrath.
Be merciful to me, Lord, for I am
    faint;
  O Lord, heal me, for my bones
    are in agony.
My soul is in anguish.
  How long, O Lord, how long?

Turn, O Lord, and deliver me;
  save me because of your
    unfailing love.
No-one remembers you when he
    is dead.
  Who praises you from his grave?

I am worn out from groaning;
  all night long I flood my bed
    with weeping
  and drench my couch with
    tears.
My eyes grow weak with sorrow;
  they fail because of all my foes.

Away from me, all you who do evil,
  for the Lord has heard my
    weeping.
The Lord has heard my cry for
    mercy;
  the Lord accepts my prayer.
All my enemies will be ashamed
    and dismayed;
  they will turn back in sudden
    disgrace.

# Psalm 7

*A* shiggaion *of David, which he sang
to the* Lord *concerning Cush, a
Benjamite.*

O Lord my God, I take refuge in
    you;
  save and deliver me from all
    who pursue me,
or they will tear me like a lion
  and rip me to pieces with no-
    one to rescue me.

O Lord my God, if I have done
    this
  and there is guilt on my
    hands—
if I have done evil to him who is
    at peace with me
  or without cause have robbed
    my foe—
then let my enemy pursue and
    overtake me;
  let him trample my life to the
    ground
  and make me sleep in the dust.
                                    *Selah*

Arise, O Lord, in your anger;
  rise up against the rage of my
    enemies.
  Awake, my God; decree justice.
Let the assembled peoples gather
    round you.
  Rule over them from on high;
  let the Lord judge the peoples.
Judge me, O Lord, according to
    my righteousness,
  according to my integrity, O
    Most High.

O righteous God,
  who searches minds and hearts,
bring to an end the violence of the
    wicked
  and make the righteous secure.

My shield is God Most High,
  who saves the upright in
    heart.
God is a righteous judge,
  a God who expresses his wrath
    every day.
If he does not relent,
  he will sharpen his sword;
  he will bend and string his
    bow.
He has prepared his deadly
    weapons;
  he makes ready his flaming
    arrows.

He who is pregnant with evil
  and conceives trouble gives
    birth to disillusionment.
He who digs a hole and scoops it
    out
  falls into the pit he has made.
The trouble he causes recoils on
    himself;
  his violence comes down on his
    own head.

I will give thanks to the LORD
    because of his righteousness
  and will sing praise to the
    name of the LORD Most
    High.

∾

## Psalm 8

*For the director of music. According to*
*gittith. A psalm of David.*

O LORD, our Lord,
  how majestic is your name in
    all the earth!

You have set your glory
  above the heavens.
From the lips of children and
    infants
  you have ordained praise
because of your enemies,
  to silence the foe and the
    avenger.

When I consider your heavens,
  the work of your fingers,
the moon and the stars,
  which you have set in place,
what is man that you are mindful
    of him,
  the son of man that you care for
    him?
You made him a little lower than
    the heavenly beings
  and crowned him with glory
    and honour.

You made him ruler over the
    works of your hands;
  you put everything under his
    feet:
all flocks and herds,
  and the beasts of the field,
the birds of the air,
  and the fish of the sea,
  all that swim the paths of the
    seas.

O LORD, our Lord,
  how majestic is your name in
    all the earth!

~

## Psalm 9

*For the director of music. To the tune of "The Death of the Son". A psalm of David.*

I will praise you, O LORD, with all
    my heart;
  I will tell of all your wonders.
I will be glad and rejoice in you;
  I will sing praise to your name,
    O Most High.

My enemies turn back;
  they stumble and perish before
    you.
For you have upheld my right
    and my cause;
  you have sat on your throne,
    judging righteously.
You have rebuked the nations and
    destroyed the wicked;
  you have blotted out their name
    for ever and ever.
Endless ruin has overtaken the
    enemy,
  you have uprooted their cities;
  even the memory of them has
    perished.

The LORD reigns for ever;
  he has established his throne
    for judgment.
He will judge the world in
    righteousness;

he will govern the peoples with
    justice.
The LORD is a refuge for the
    oppressed,
  a stronghold in times of
    trouble.
Those who know your name will
    trust in you,
  for you, LORD, have never forsaken
    those who seek you.

Sing praises to the LORD,
    enthroned in Zion;
  proclaim among the nations
    what he has done.
For he who avenges blood
    remembers;
  he does not ignore the cry of
    the afflicted.

O LORD, see how my enemies
    persecute me!
  Have mercy and lift me up
    from the gates of death,
that I may declare your praises
  in the gates of the Daughter of
    Zion
  and there rejoice in your
    salvation.
The nations have fallen into the
    pit they have dug;
  their feet are caught in the net
    they have hidden.
The LORD is known by his justice;
  the wicked are ensnared by the
    work of their hands.
                    *Higgaion. Selah*

The wicked return to the grave,
  all the nations that forget God.

But the needy will not always be
forgotten,
  nor the hope of the afflicted
  ever perish.

Arise, O LORD, let not man
triumph;
  let the nations be judged in
  your presence.
Strike them with terror, O LORD;
  let the nations know they are
  but men.                    *Selah*

~

## Psalm 10

Why, O LORD, do you stand far
off?
  Why do you hide yourself in
  times of trouble?

In his arrogance the wicked man
hunts down the weak,
  who are caught in the schemes
  he devises.
He boasts of the cravings of his
heart;
  he blesses the greedy and
  reviles the LORD.
In his pride the wicked does not
seek him;
  in all his thoughts there is no
  room for God.
His ways are always prosperous;
  he is haughty and your laws are
  far from him;
  he sneers at all his enemies.
He says to himself, "Nothing will
shake me;

I'll always be happy and never
have trouble."
His mouth is full of curses and
lies and threats;
  trouble and evil are under his
  tongue.
He lies in wait near the villages;
  from ambush he murders the
  innocent,
  watching in secret for his
  victims.
He lies in wait like a lion in cover;
  he lies in wait to catch the
  helpless;
  he catches the helpless and
  drags them off in his net.
His victims are crushed, they
collapse;
  they fall under his strength.
He says to himself, "God has
forgotten;
  he covers his face and never sees."

Arise, LORD! Lift up your hand, O
God.
  Do not forget the helpless.
Why does the wicked man revile
God?
  Why does he say to himself,
  "He won't call me to account"?
But you, O God, do see trouble
and grief;
  you consider it to take it in
  hand.
The victim commits himself to
you;
  you are the helper of the
  fatherless.
Break the arm of the wicked and
evil man;

call him to account for his
wickedness
that would not be found out.

The LORD is King for ever and
ever;
the nations will perish from his
land.
You hear, O LORD, the desire of
the afflicted;
you encourage them, and you
listen to their cry,
defending the fatherless and the
oppressed,
in order that man, who is of the
earth, may terrify no more.

~

## Psalm 11
*For the director of music. Of David.*

In the LORD I take refuge.
How then can you say to me:
"Flee like a bird to your
mountain.
For look, the wicked bend their
bows;
they set their arrows against the
strings
to shoot from the shadows
at the upright in heart.
When the foundations are being
destroyed,
what can the righteous do?"

The LORD is in his holy temple;
the LORD is on his heavenly
throne.
He observes the sons of men;

his eyes examine them.
The LORD examines the righteous,
but the wicked and those who
love violence
his soul hates.
On the wicked he will rain
fiery coals and burning sulphur;
a scorching wind will be their
lot.

For the LORD is righteous,
he loves justice;
upright men will see his face.

~

## Psalm 12
*For the director of music. According to
sheminith. A psalm of David.*

Help, LORD, for the godly are no
more;
the faithful have vanished from
among men.
Everyone lies to his neighbour;
their flattering lips speak with
deception.

May the LORD cut off all flattering
lips
and every boastful tongue
that says, "We will triumph with
our tongues;
we own our lips—who is our
master?"

"Because of the oppression of the
weak
and the groaning of the needy,
I will now arise," says the LORD.

"I will protect them from those
who malign them."
And the words of the LORD are
flawless,
like silver refined in a furnace
of clay,
purified seven times.

O LORD, you will keep us safe
and protect us from such
people for ever.
The wicked freely strut about
when what is vile is honoured
among men.

~

## Psalm 13
*For the director of music. A psalm of
David.*

How long, O LORD? Will you
forget me for ever?
How long will you hide your
face from me?
How long must I wrestle with my
thoughts
and every day have sorrow in
my heart?
How long will my enemy
triumph over me?

Look on me and answer, O LORD
my God.
Give light to my eyes, or I will
sleep in death;
my enemy will say, "I have
overcome him,"
and my foes will rejoice when I
fall.

But I trust in your unfailing love;
my heart rejoices in your
salvation.
I will sing to the LORD,
for he has been good to me.

~

## Psalm 14
*For the director of music. Of David.*

The fool says in his heart,
"There is no God."
They are corrupt, their deeds are
vile;
there is no-one who does good.

The LORD looks down from heaven
on the sons of men
to see if there are any who
understand,
any who seek God.
All have turned aside,
they have together become
corrupt;
there is no-one who does good,
not even one.

Will evildoers never learn—
those who devour my people as
men eat bread
and who do not call on the
LORD?
There they are, overwhelmed with
dread,
for God is present in the
company of the righteous.
You evildoers frustrate the plans
of the poor,
but the LORD is their refuge.

Oh, that salvation for Israel would
come out of Zion!
When the LORD restores the
fortunes of his people,
let Jacob rejoice and Israel be
glad!

~

## Psalm 15
*A psalm of David.*

LORD, who may dwell in your
sanctuary?
Who may live on your holy
hill?

He whose walk is blameless
and who does what is
righteous,
who speaks the truth from his
heart
and has no slander on his
tongue,
who does his neighbour no
wrong
and casts no slur on his fellow-
man,
who despises a vile man
but honours those who fear the
LORD,
who keeps his oath
even when it hurts,
who lends his money without
usury
and does not accept a bribe
against the innocent.

He who does these things
will never be shaken.

## Psalm 16
*A miktam of David.*

Keep me safe, O God,
for in you I take refuge.

I said to the LORD, "You are my
Lord;
apart from you I have no good
thing."
As for the saints who are in the
land,
they are the glorious ones in
whom is all my delight.
The sorrows of those will increase
who run after other gods.
I will not pour out their libations
of blood
or take up their names on my
lips.

LORD, you have assigned me my
portion and my cup;
you have made my lot secure.
The boundary lines have fallen for
me in pleasant places;
surely I have a delightful
inheritance.

I will praise the LORD, who
counsels me;
even at night my heart instructs
me.
I have set the LORD always before
me.
Because he is at my right hand,
I shall not be shaken.

Therefore my heart is glad and
my tongue rejoices;

my body also will rest secure,
because you will not abandon me
    to the grave,
    nor will you let your Holy One
      see decay.
You have made known to me the
    path of life;
    you will fill me with joy in
      your presence,
    with eternal pleasures at your
      right hand.

∼

## Psalm 17
*A prayer of David.*

Hear, O LORD, my righteous plea;
    listen to my cry.
Give ear to my prayer—
    it does not rise from deceitful
      lips.
May my vindication come from
    you;
    may your eyes see what is
      right.

Though you probe my heart and
    examine me at night,
    though you test me, you will
      find nothing;
    I have resolved that my mouth
      will not sin.
As for the deeds of men—
    by the word of your lips
I have kept myself
    from the ways of the violent.
My steps have held to your
    paths;
    my feet have not slipped.

I call on you, O God, for you will
    answer me;
    give ear to me and hear my
      prayer.
Show the wonder of your great
    love,
    you who save by your right
      hand
    those who take refuge in you
      from their foes.
Keep me as the apple of your eye;
    hide me in the shadow of your
      wings
from the wicked who assail me,
    from my mortal enemies who
      surround me.

They close up their callous hearts,
    and their mouths speak with
      arrogance.
They have tracked me down, they
    now surround me,
    with eyes alert, to throw me to
      the ground.
They are like a lion hungry for
    prey,
    like a great lion crouching in
      cover.

Rise up, O LORD, confront them,
    bring them down;
    rescue me from the wicked by
      your sword.
O LORD, by your hand save me
    from such men,
    from men of this world whose
      reward is in this life.

You still the hunger of those you
    cherish;

their sons have plenty,
and they store up wealth for
their children.
And I—in righteousness I shall see
your face;
when I awake, I shall be
satisfied with seeing your
likeness.

~

## Psalm 18

*For the director of music. Of David the
servant of the LORD. He sang to the
LORD the words of this song when the
LORD delivered him from the hand of all
his enemies and from the hand of Saul.
He said:*

I love you, O LORD, my strength.

The LORD is my rock, my fortress
and my deliverer;
my God is my rock, in whom I
take refuge.
He is my shield and the horn of
my salvation, my
stronghold.
I call to the LORD, who is worthy
of praise,
and I am saved from my
enemies.

The cords of death entangled me;
the torrents of destruction
overwhelmed me.
The cords of the grave coiled
around me;
the snares of death confronted
me.

In my distress I called to the LORD;
I cried to my God for help.
From his temple he heard my
voice;
my cry came before him, into
his ears.

The earth trembled and quaked,
and the foundations of the
mountains shook;
they trembled because he was
angry.
Smoke rose from his nostrils;
consuming fire came from his
mouth,
burning coals blazed out of it.
He parted the heavens and came
down;
dark clouds were under his
feet.
He mounted the cherubim and
flew;
he soared on the wings of the
wind.
He made darkness his covering,
his canopy around him—
the dark rain clouds of the sky.
Out of the brightness of his
presence clouds advanced,
with hailstones and bolts of
lightning.
The LORD thundered from heaven;
the voice of the Most High
resounded.
He shot his arrows and scattered
ˌthe enemiesˌ,
great bolts of lightning and
routed them.
The valleys of the sea were
exposed

and the foundations of the earth
    laid bare
at your rebuke, O LORD,
    at the blast of breath from your
      nostrils.

He reached down from on high
    and took hold of me;
    he drew me out of deep waters.
He rescued me from my powerful
    enemy,
    from my foes, who were too
      strong for me.
They confronted me in the day of
    my disaster,
    but the LORD was my support.
He brought me out into a
    spacious place;
    he rescued me because he
      delighted in me.

The LORD has dealt with me
    according to my
    righteousness;
    according to the cleanness of my
      hands he has rewarded me.
For I have kept the ways of the
    LORD;
    I have not done evil by turning
      from my God.
All his laws are before me;
    I have not turned away from
      his decrees.
I have been blameless before him
    and have kept myself from sin.
The LORD has rewarded me
    according to my
    righteousness,
    according to the cleanness of
      my hands in his sight.

To the faithful you show yourself
    faithful,
    to the blameless you show
      yourself blameless,
to the pure you show yourself
    pure
    but to the crooked you show
      yourself shrewd.
You save the humble
    but bring low those whose eyes
      are haughty.
You, O LORD, keep my lamp
    burning;
    my God turns my darkness into
      light.
With your help I can advance
    against a troop;
    with my God I can scale a wall.

As for God, his way is perfect;
    the word of the LORD is
      flawless.
He is a shield
    for all who take refuge in him.
For who is God besides the LORD?
    And who is the Rock except
      our God?
It is God who arms me with
    strength
    and makes my way perfect.
He makes my feet like the feet of
    a deer;
    he enables me to stand on the
      heights.
He trains my hands for battle;
    my arms can bend a bow of
      bronze.
You give me your shield of
    victory,
    and your right hand sustains me;

you stoop down to make me
great.
You broaden the path beneath me,
so that my ankles do not turn
over.

I pursued my enemies and
overtook them;
I did not turn back till they
were destroyed.
I crushed them so that they could
not rise;
they fell beneath my feet.
You armed me with strength for
battle;
you made my adversaries bow
at my feet.
You made my enemies turn their
backs in flight,
and I destroyed my foes.
They cried for help, but there was
no-one to save them—
to the Lord, but he did not answer.
I beat them as fine as dust borne
on the wind;
I poured them out like mud in
the streets.

You have delivered me from the
attacks of the people;
you have made me the head of
nations;
people I did not know are
subject to me.
As soon as they hear me, they
obey me;
foreigners cringe before me.
They all lose heart;
they come trembling from their
strongholds.

The Lord lives! Praise be to my
Rock!
Exalted be God my Saviour!
He is the God who avenges me,
who subdues nations under me,
who saves me from my
enemies.
You exalted me above my foes;
from violent men you rescued
me.
Therefore I will praise you among
the nations, O Lord;
I will sing praises to your
name.
He gives his king great victories;
he shows unfailing kindness to
his anointed,
to David and his descendants
for ever.

~

## Psalm 19

*For the director of music. A psalm of
David.*

The heavens declare the glory of
God;
the skies proclaim the work of
his hands.
Day after day they pour forth
speech;
night after night they display
knowledge.
There is no speech or language
where their voice is not heard.
Their voice goes out into all the
earth,
their words to the ends of the
world.

In the heavens he has pitched a
tent for the sun,
which is like a bridegroom
coming forth from his
pavilion,
like a champion rejoicing to run
his course.
It rises at one end of the heavens
and makes its circuit to the
other;
nothing is hidden from its heat.

The law of the LORD is perfect,
reviving the soul.
The statutes of the LORD are
trustworthy,
making wise the simple.
The precepts of the LORD are right,
giving joy to the heart.
The commands of the LORD are
radiant,
giving light to the eyes.
The fear of the LORD is pure,
enduring for ever.
The ordinances of the LORD are
sure
and altogether righteous.
They are more precious than gold,
than much pure gold;
they are sweeter than honey,
than honey from the comb.
By them is your servant warned;
in keeping them there is great
reward.

Who can discern his errors?
Forgive my hidden faults.
Keep your servant also from
wilful sins;
may they not rule over me.

Then will I be blameless,
innocent of great transgression.

May the words of my mouth and
the meditation of my heart
be pleasing in your sight,
O LORD, my Rock and my
Redeemer.

~

## Psalm 20

*For the director of music. A psalm of
David.*

May the LORD answer you when
you are in distress;
may the name of the God of
Jacob protect you.
May he send you help from the
sanctuary
and grant you support from
Zion.
May he remember all your
sacrifices
and accept your burnt offerings.
*Selah*
May he give you the desire of
your heart
and make all your plans
succeed.
We will shout for joy when you
are victorious
and will lift up our banners in
the name of our God.
May the LORD grant all your
requests.

Now I know that the LORD saves
his anointed;

he answers him from his holy
heaven
with the saving power of his
right hand.
Some trust in chariots and some
in horses,
but we trust in the name of the
LORD our God.
They are brought to their knees
and fall,
but we rise up and stand firm.

O LORD, save the king!
Answer us when we call!

∾

## Psalm 21

*For the director of music. A psalm of
David.*

O LORD, the king rejoices in your
strength.
How great is his joy in the
victories you give!
You have granted him the desire
of his heart
and have not withheld the
request of his lips.     *Selah*
You welcomed him with rich
blessings
and placed a crown of pure
gold on his head.
He asked you for life, and you
gave it to him—
length of days, for ever and ever.
Through the victories you gave,
his glory is great;
you have bestowed on him
splendour and majesty.

Surely you have granted him
eternal blessings
and made him glad with the joy
of your presence.
For the king trusts in the LORD;
through the unfailing love of
the Most High
he will not be shaken.

Your hand will lay hold on all
your enemies;
your right hand will seize your
foes.
At the time of your appearing
you will make them like a fiery
furnace.
In his wrath the LORD will
swallow them up,
and his fire will consume them.
You will destroy their descendants
from the earth,
their posterity from mankind.
Though they plot evil against you
and devise wicked schemes,
they cannot succeed;
for you will make them turn their
backs
when you aim at them with
drawn bow.

Be exalted, O LORD, in your
strength;
we will sing and praise your
might.

∾

## Psalm 22

*For the director of music. To the tune
of "The Doe of the Morning". A psalm
of David.*

My God, my God, why have you
forsaken me?
Why are you so far from saving
me,
so far from the words of my
groaning?
O my God, I cry out by day, but
you do not answer,
by night, and am not silent.

Yet you are enthroned as the Holy
One;
you are the praise of Israel.
In you our fathers put their trust;
they trusted and you delivered
them.
They cried to you and were saved;
in you they trusted and were
not disappointed.

But I am a worm and not a man,
scorned by men and despised
by the people.
All who see me mock me;
they hurl insults, shaking their
heads:
"He trusts in the LORD;
let the LORD rescue him.
Let him deliver him,
since he delights in him."

Yet you brought me out of the
womb;
you made me trust in you
even at my mother's breast.

From birth I was cast upon you;
from my mother's womb
you have been my God.
Do not be far from me,
for trouble is near
and there is no-one to help.

Many bulls surround me;
strong bulls of Bashan encircle
me.
Roaring lions tearing their prey
open their mouths wide against
me.
I am poured out like water,
and all my bones are out of joint.
My heart has turned to wax;
it has melted away within me.
My strength is dried up like a
potsherd,
and my tongue sticks to the
roof of my mouth;
you lay me in the dust of
death.
Dogs have surrounded me;
a band of evil men has
encircled me,
they have pierced my hands
and my feet.
I can count all my bones;
people stare and gloat over me.
They divide my garments among
them
and cast lots for my clothing.

But you, O LORD, be not far off;
O my Strength, come quickly to
help me.
Deliver my life from the sword,
my precious life from the
power of the dogs.

Rescue me from the mouth of the
    lions;
    save me from the horns of the
      wild oxen.

I will declare your name to my
    brothers;
    in the congregation I will praise
      you.
You who fear the LORD, praise
    him!
    All you descendants of Jacob,
      honour him!
    Revere him, all you descendants
      of Israel!
For he has not despised or
    disdained
    the suffering of the afflicted
      one;
he has not hidden his face from
    him
    but has listened to his cry for
      help.

From you comes the theme of my
    praise in the great
    assembly;
    before those who fear you will I
      fulfil my vows.
The poor will eat and be satisfied;
    they who seek the LORD will
      praise him—
    may your hearts live for ever!
All the ends of the earth
    will remember and turn to the
      LORD,
and all the families of the nations
    will bow down before him,
for dominion belongs to the LORD
    and he rules over the nations.

All the rich of the earth will feast
    and worship;
    all who go down to the dust
      will kneel before him—
    those who cannot keep
      themselves alive.
Posterity will serve him;
    future generations will be told
      about the Lord.
They will proclaim his
    righteousness
    to a people yet unborn—
    for he has done it.

## Psalm 23
*A psalm of David.*

The LORD is my shepherd, I shall
    not be in want.
    He makes me lie down in green
      pastures,
he leads me beside quiet waters,
    he restores my soul.
He guides me in paths of
    righteousness
    for his name's sake.
Even though I walk
    through the valley of the
      shadow of death,
I will fear no evil,
    for you are with me;
your rod and your staff,
    they comfort me.

You prepare a table before me
    in the presence of my enemies.
You anoint my head with oil;
    my cup overflows.

Surely goodness and love will
    follow me
  all the days of my life,
and I will dwell in the house of
    the LORD
  for ever.

~

## Psalm 24
*Of David. A psalm.*

The earth is the LORD's, and
    everything in it,
  the world, and all who live in
    it;
for he founded it upon the seas
  and established it upon the
    waters.

Who may ascend the hill of the
    LORD?
  Who may stand in his holy
    place?
He who has clean hands and a
    pure heart,
  who does not lift up his soul to
    an idol
  or swear by what is false.
He will receive blessing from the
    LORD
  and vindication from God his
    Saviour.
Such is the generation of those
    who seek him,
  who seek your face, O God of
    Jacob.     *Selah*

Lift up your heads, O you gates;
  be lifted up, you ancient doors,

that the King of glory may
    come in.
Who is this King of glory?
  The LORD strong and mighty,
  the LORD mighty in battle.
Lift up your heads, O you gates;
  lift them up, you ancient doors,
  that the King of glory may
    come in.
Who is he, this King of glory?
  The LORD Almighty—
  he is the King of glory.     *Selah*

~

## Psalm 25
*Of David.*

To you, O LORD, I lift up my soul;
  in you I trust, O my God.
Do not let me be put to shame,
  nor let my enemies triumph
    over me.
No-one whose hope is in you
  will ever be put to shame,
but they will be put to shame
  who are treacherous without
    excuse.

Show me your ways, O LORD,
  teach me your paths;
guide me in your truth and teach me,
  for you are God my Saviour,
  and my hope is in you all day
    long.
Remember, O LORD, your great
    mercy and love,
  for they are from of old.
Remember not the sins of my
    youth

and my rebellious ways;
according to your love remember
me,
for you are good, O LORD.

Good and upright is the LORD;
therefore he instructs sinners in
his ways.
He guides the humble in what is
right
and teaches them his way.
All the ways of the LORD are
loving and faithful
for those who keep the
demands of his covenant.
For the sake of your name,
O LORD,
forgive my iniquity, though it is
great.
Who, then, is the man that fears
the LORD?
He will instruct him in the way
chosen for him.
He will spend his days in
prosperity,
and his descendants will inherit
the land.
The LORD confides in those who
fear him;
he makes his covenant known
to them.
My eyes are ever on the LORD,
for only he will release my feet
from the snare.

Turn to me and be gracious to
me,
for I am lonely and afflicted.
The troubles of my heart have
multiplied;

free me from my anguish.
Look upon my affliction and my
distress
and take away all my sins.
See how my enemies have
increased
and how fiercely they hate me!
Guard my life and rescue me;
let me not be put to shame,
for I take refuge in you.
May integrity and uprightness
protect me,
because my hope is in you.

Redeem Israel, O God,
from all their troubles!

∾

## Psalm 26
*Of David.*

Vindicate me, O LORD,
for I have led a blameless life;
I have trusted in the LORD
without wavering.
Test me, O LORD, and try me,
examine my heart and my
mind;
for your love is ever before me,
and I walk continually in your
truth.
I do not sit with deceitful men,
nor do I consort with
hypocrites;
I abhor the assembly of evildoers
and refuse to sit with the
wicked.
I wash my hands in innocence,
and go about your altar, O LORD,

proclaiming aloud your praise
and telling of all your
wonderful deeds.
I love the house where you live,
O LORD,
the place where your glory
dwells.

Do not take away my soul along
with sinners,
my life with bloodthirsty men,
in whose hands are wicked
schemes,
whose right hands are full of
bribes.
But I lead a blameless life;
redeem me and be merciful to
me.

My feet stand on level ground;
in the great assembly I will
praise the LORD.

∾

# Psalm 27
*Of David.*

The LORD is my light and my
salvation—
whom shall I fear?
The LORD is the stronghold of my
life—
of whom shall I be afraid?
When evil men advance against
me
to devour my flesh,
when my enemies and my foes
attack me,
they will stumble and fall.

Though an army besiege me,
my heart will not fear;
though war break out against me,
even then will I be confident.

One thing I ask of the LORD,
this is what I seek:
that I may dwell in the house of
the LORD
all the days of my life,
to gaze upon the beauty of the
LORD
and to seek him in his temple.
For in the day of trouble
he will keep me safe in his
dwelling;
he will hide me in the shelter of
his tabernacle
and set me high upon a rock.
Then my head will be exalted
above the enemies who
surround me;
at his tabernacle will I sacrifice
with shouts of joy;
I will sing and make music to
the LORD.

Hear my voice when I call,
O LORD;
be merciful to me and answer
me.
My heart says of you, "Seek his
face!"
Your face, LORD, I will seek.
Do not hide your face from me,
do not turn your servant away
in anger;
you have been my helper.
Do not reject me or forsake me,
O God my Saviour.

Though my father and mother
    forsake me,
  the LORD will receive me.
Teach me your way, O LORD;
  lead me in a straight path
  because of my oppressors.
Do not hand me over to the desire
    of my foes,
  for false witnesses rise up
    against me,
  breathing out violence.

I am still confident of this:
  I will see the goodness of the LORD
  in the land of the living.
Wait for the LORD;
  be strong and take heart
  and wait for the LORD.

## Psalm 28
*Of David.*

To you I call, O LORD my Rock;
  do not turn a deaf ear to me.
For if you remain silent,
  I shall be like those who have
    gone down to the pit.
Hear my cry for mercy
  as I call to you for help,
as I lift up my hands
  towards your Most Holy Place.

Do not drag me away with the
    wicked,
  with those who do evil,
who speak cordially with their
    neighbours
  but harbour malice in their hearts.

Repay them for their deeds
  and for their evil work;
repay them for what their hands
    have done
  and bring back upon them what
    they deserve.
Since they show no regard for the
    works of the LORD
  and what his hands have done,
he will tear them down
  and never build them up again.

Praise be to the LORD,
  for he has heard my cry for mercy.
The LORD is my strength and my
    shield;
  my heart trusts in him, and I
    am helped.
My heart leaps for joy
  and I will give thanks to him in
    song.

The LORD is the strength of his
    people,
  a fortress of salvation for his
    anointed one.
Save your people and bless your
    inheritance;
  be their shepherd and carry
    them for ever.

## Psalm 29
*A psalm of David.*

Ascribe to the LORD, O mighty
    ones,
  ascribe to the LORD glory and
    strength.

Ascribe to the LORD the glory due
    to his name;
  worship the LORD in the
    splendour of his holiness.

The voice of the LORD is over the
    waters;
  the God of glory thunders,
  the LORD thunders over the
    mighty waters.
The voice of the LORD is powerful;
  the voice of the LORD is
    majestic.
The voice of the LORD breaks the
    cedars;
  the LORD breaks in pieces the
    cedars of Lebanon.
He makes Lebanon skip like a
    calf,
  Sirion like a young wild ox.
The voice of the LORD strikes
    with flashes of lightning.
The voice of the LORD shakes the
    desert;
  the LORD shakes the Desert of
    Kadesh.
The voice of the LORD twists the
    oaks
  and strips the forests bare.
And in his temple all cry,
    "Glory!"

The LORD sits enthroned over the
    flood;
  the LORD is enthroned as King
    for ever.
The LORD gives strength to his
    people;
  the LORD blesses his people with
    peace.

# Psalm 30

*A psalm. A song. For the dedication of
the temple. Of David.*

I will exalt you, O LORD,
  for you lifted me out of the depths
  and did not let my enemies
    gloat over me.
O LORD my God, I called to you
    for help
  and you healed me.
O LORD, you brought me up from
    the grave;
  you spared me from going
    down into the pit.

Sing to the LORD, you saints of his;
  praise his holy name.
For his anger lasts only a moment,
  but his favour lasts a lifetime;
weeping may remain for a night,
  but rejoicing comes in the
    morning.

When I felt secure, I said,
  "I shall never be shaken."
O LORD, when you favoured me,
  you made my mountain stand
    firm;
but when you hid your face,
  I was dismayed.

To you, O LORD, I called;
  to the Lord I cried for mercy:
"What gain is there in my
    destruction,
  in my going down into the pit?
Will the dust praise you?
  Will it proclaim your
    faithfulness?

Hear, O LORD, and be merciful to
me;
O LORD, be my help."

You turned my wailing into
dancing;
you removed my sackcloth and
clothed me with joy,
that my heart may sing to you
and not be silent.
O LORD my God, I will give you
thanks for ever.

≈

## Psalm 31

*For the director of music. A psalm of
David.*

In you, O LORD, I have taken
refuge;
let me never be put to shame;
deliver me in your
righteousness.
Turn your ear to me,
come quickly to my rescue;
be my rock of refuge,
a strong fortress to save me.
Since you are my rock and my
fortress,
for the sake of your name lead
and guide me.
Free me from the trap that is set
for me,
for you are my refuge.
Into your hands I commit my
spirit;
redeem me, O LORD, the God of
truth.

I hate those who cling to
worthless idols;
I trust in the LORD.
I will be glad and rejoice in your
love,
for you saw my affliction
and knew the anguish of my
soul.
You have not handed me over to
the enemy
but have set my feet in a
spacious place.

Be merciful to me, O LORD, for I
am in distress;
my eyes grow weak with sorrow,
my soul and my body with
grief.
My life is consumed by anguish
and my years by groaning;
my strength fails because of my
affliction,
and my bones grow weak.
Because of all my enemies,
I am the utter contempt of my
neighbours;
I am a dread to my friends—
those who see me on the street
flee from me.
I am forgotten by them as though
I were dead;
I have become like broken
pottery.
For I hear the slander of many;
there is terror on every side;
they conspire against me
and plot to take my life.

But I trust in you, O LORD;
I say, "You are my God."

My times are in your hands;
    deliver me from my enemies
    and from those who pursue me.
Let your face shine on your
        servant;
    save me in your unfailing love.
Let me not be put to shame,
        O Lord,
    for I have cried out to you;
but let the wicked be put to
        shame
    and lie silent in the grave.
Let their lying lips be silenced,
    for with pride and contempt
    they speak arrogantly against
        the righteous.

How great is your goodness,
    which you have stored up for
        those who fear you,
which you bestow in the sight of
        men
    on those who take refuge in
        you.
In the shelter of your presence
        you hide them
    from the intrigues of men;
in your dwelling you keep them
        safe
    from accusing tongues.

Praise be to the Lord,
    for he showed his wonderful
        love to me
    when I was in a besieged city.
In my alarm I said,
    "I am cut off from your
        sight!"
Yet you heard my cry for mercy
    when I called to you for help.

Love the Lord, all his saints!
    The Lord preserves the faithful,
    but the proud he pays back in full.
Be strong and take heart,
    all you who hope in the Lord.

~

## Psalm 32
*Of David. A* maskil.

Blessed is he
    whose transgressions are
        forgiven,
    whose sins are covered.
Blessed is the man
    whose sin the Lord does not
        count against him
    and in whose spirit is no deceit.

When I kept silent,
    my bones wasted away
    through my groaning all day long.
For day and night
    your hand was heavy upon me;
my strength was sapped
    as in the heat of summer.    *Selah*
Then I acknowledged my sin to
        you
    and did not cover up my iniquity.
I said, "I will confess
    my transgressions to the
        Lord"—
and you forgave
    the guilt of my sin.    *Selah*

Therefore let everyone who is
        godly pray to you
    while you may be found;
surely when the mighty waters rise,

they will not reach him.
You are my hiding-place;
　　you will protect me from
　　　trouble
　　and surround me with songs of
　　　deliverance.　　　　　*Selah*

I will instruct you and teach you
　　　in the way you should go;
　　I will counsel you and watch
　　　over you.
Do not be like the horse or the
　　　mule,
　　which have no understanding
but must be controlled by bit and
　　　bridle
　　or they will not come to you.
Many are the woes of the wicked,
　　but the LORD's unfailing love
　　surrounds the man who trusts
　　　in him.

Rejoice in the LORD and be glad,
　　　you righteous;
　　sing, all you who are upright in
　　　heart!

～

## Psalm 33

Sing joyfully to the LORD, you
　　　righteous;
　　it is fitting for the upright to
　　　praise him.
Praise the LORD with the harp;
　　make music to him on the ten-
　　　stringed lyre.
Sing to him a new song;
　　play skilfully, and shout for joy.

For the word of the LORD is right
　　　and true;
　　he is faithful in all he does.
The LORD loves righteousness and
　　　justice;
　　the earth is full of his unfailing
　　　love.

By the word of the LORD were the
　　　heavens made,
　　their starry host by the breath
　　　of his mouth.
He gathers the waters of the sea
　　　into jars;
　　he puts the deep into
　　　storehouses.
Let all the earth fear the LORD;
　　let all the people of the world
　　　revere him.
For he spoke, and it came to be;
　　he commanded, and it stood
　　　firm.
The LORD foils the plans of the
　　　nations;
　　he thwarts the purposes of the
　　　peoples.
But the plans of the LORD stand
　　　firm for ever,
　　the purposes of his heart
　　　through all generations.

Blessed is the nation whose God
　　　is the LORD,
　　the people he chose for his
　　　inheritance.
From heaven the LORD looks down
　　and sees all mankind;
　　from his dwelling-place he
　　　watches
　　all who live on earth—

he who forms the hearts of all,
  who considers everything they do.
No king is saved by the size of
    his army;
  no warrior escapes by his great
    strength.
A horse is a vain hope for
    deliverance;
  despite all its great strength it
    cannot save.
But the eyes of the LORD are on
    those who fear him,
  on those whose hope is in his
    unfailing love,
to deliver them from death
  and keep them alive in famine.

We wait in hope for the LORD;
  he is our help and our shield.
In him our hearts rejoice,
  for we trust in his holy name.
May your unfailing love rest upon
    us, O LORD,
  even as we put our hope in
    you.

~

# Psalm 34

*Of David. When he pretended to be
insane before Abimelech, who drove
him away, and he left.*

I will extol the LORD at all times;
  his praise will always be on my
    lips.
My soul will boast in the LORD;
  let the afflicted hear and rejoice.
Glorify the LORD with me:
  let us exalt his name together.

I sought the LORD, and he
    answered me;
  he delivered me from all my
    fears.
Those who look to him are
    radiant;
  their faces are never covered
    with shame.
This poor man called, and the
    LORD heard him;
  he saved him out of all his
    troubles.
The angel of the LORD encamps
    around those who fear
    him,
  and he delivers them.

Taste and see that the LORD is
    good;
  blessed is the man who takes
    refuge in him.
Fear the LORD, you his saints,
  for those who fear him lack
    nothing.
The lions may grow weak and
    hungry,
  but those who seek the LORD
    lack no good thing.

Come, my children, listen to me;
  I will teach you the fear of the
    LORD.
Whoever of you loves life
  and desires to see many good
    days,
keep your tongue from evil
  and your lips from speaking
    lies.
Turn from evil and do good;
  seek peace and pursue it.

The eyes of the LORD are on the
    righteous
  and his ears are attentive to
    their cry;
the face of the LORD is against
    those who do evil,
  to cut off the memory of them
    from the earth.

The righteous cry out, and the
    LORD hears them;
  he delivers them from all their
    troubles.
The LORD is close to the broken-
    hearted
  and saves those who are
    crushed in spirit.

A righteous man may have many
    troubles,
  but the LORD delivers him from
    them all;
he protects all his bones,
  not one of them will be broken.

Evil will slay the wicked;
  the foes of the righteous will be
    condemned.
The LORD redeems his servants;
  no-one will be condemned who
    takes refuge in him.

∾

# Psalm 35
*Of David.*

Contend, O LORD, with those who
    contend with me;
  fight against those who fight
    against me.

Take up shield and buckler;
  arise and come to my aid.
Brandish spear and javelin
  against those who pursue
    me.
Say to my soul,
  "I am your salvation."

May those who seek my life
  be disgraced and put to
    shame;
may those who plot my ruin
  be turned back in dismay.
May they be like chaff before the
    wind,
  with the angel of the LORD
    driving them away;
may their path be dark and
    slippery,
  with the angel of the LORD
    pursuing them.
Since they hid their net for me
    without cause
  and without cause dug a pit for
    me,
may ruin overtake them by
    surprise—
  may the net they hid entangle
    them,
  may they fall into the pit, to
    their ruin.
Then my soul will rejoice in the
    LORD
  and delight in his salvation.
My whole being will exclaim,
  "Who is like you, O LORD?
You rescue the poor from those
    too strong for them,
  the poor and needy from those
    who rob them."

Ruthless witnesses come forward;
  they question me on things I
    know nothing about.
They repay me evil for good
  and leave my soul forlorn.
Yet when they were ill, I put on
    sackcloth
  and humbled myself with
    fasting.
When my prayers returned to me
    unanswered,
  I went about mourning
  as though for my friend or
    brother.
I bowed my head in grief
  as though weeping for my
    mother.
But when I stumbled, they
    gathered in glee;
  attackers gathered against me
    when I was unaware.
  They slandered me without
    ceasing.
Like the ungodly they maliciously
    mocked;
  they gnashed their teeth at me.
O Lord, how long will you look
    on?
  Rescue my life from their
    ravages,
  my precious life from these
    lions.
I will give you thanks in the great
    assembly;
  among throngs of people I will
    praise you.

Let not those gloat over me
  who are my enemies without
    cause;

let not those who hate me without
    reason
  maliciously wink the eye.
They do not speak peaceably,
  but devise false accusations
  against those who live quietly
    in the land.
They gape at me and say, "Aha!
    Aha!
  With our own eyes we have
    seen it."

O Lord, you have seen this; be not
    silent.
  Do not be far from me, O Lord.
Awake, and rise to my defence!
  Contend for me, my God and
    Lord.
Vindicate me in your righteousness,
    O Lord my God;
  do not let them gloat over me.
Do not let them think, "Aha, just
    what we wanted!"
  or say, "We have swallowed
    him up."

May all who gloat over my
    distress
  be put to shame and confusion;
may all who exalt themselves over
    me
  be clothed with shame and
    disgrace.
May those who delight in my
    vindication
  shout for joy and gladness;
may they always say, "The Lord
    be exalted,
  who delights in the well-being
    of his servant."

My tongue will speak of your
righteousness
and of your praises all day
long.

~

## Psalm 36

*For the director of music. Of David the
servant of the LORD.*

An oracle is within my heart
concerning the sinfulness of the
wicked:
There is no fear of God
before his eyes.
For in his own eyes he flatters
himself
too much to detect or hate his
sin.
The words of his mouth are
wicked and deceitful;
he has ceased to be wise and to
do good.
Even on his bed he plots evil;
he commits himself to a sinful
course
and does not reject what is
wrong.

Your love, O LORD, reaches to the
heavens,
your faithfulness to the skies.
Your righteousness is like the
mighty mountains,
your justice like the great deep.
O LORD, you preserve both man
and beast.
How priceless is your unfailing
love!

Both high and low among men
find refuge in the shadow of
your wings.
They feast in the abundance of
your house;
you give them drink from your
river of delights.
For with you is the fountain of life;
in your light we see light.

Continue your love to those who
know you,
your righteousness to the
upright in heart.
May the foot of the proud not
come against me,
nor the hand of the wicked
drive me away.
See how the evildoers lie fallen—
thrown down, not able to rise!

~

## Psalm 37

*Of David.*

Do not fret because of evil men
or be envious of those who do
wrong;
for like the grass they will soon
wither,
like green plants they will soon
die away.

Trust in the LORD and do good;
dwell in the land and enjoy safe
pasture.
Delight yourself in the LORD
and he will give you the desires
of your heart.

Commit your way to the LORD;
  trust in him and he will do
    this:
He will make your righteousness
    shine like the dawn,
  the justice of your cause like the
    noonday sun.

Be still before the LORD and wait
    patiently for him;
  do not fret when men succeed
    in their ways,
  when they carry out their
    wicked schemes.

Refrain from anger and turn from
    wrath;
  do not fret—it leads only to evil.
For evil men will be cut off,
  but those who hope in the LORD
    will inherit the land.

A little while, and the wicked will
    be no more;
  though you look for them, they
    will not be found.
But the meek will inherit the land
  and enjoy great peace.

The wicked plot against the
    righteous
  and gnash their teeth at them;
but the Lord laughs at the wicked,
  for he knows their day is
    coming.

The wicked draw the sword
  and bend the bow
to bring down the poor and
    needy,

to slay those whose ways are
    upright.
But their swords will pierce their
    own hearts,
  and their bows will be broken.

Better the little that the righteous
    have
  than the wealth of many
    wicked;
for the power of the wicked will
    be broken,
  but the LORD upholds the
    righteous.

The days of the blameless are
    known to the LORD,
  and their inheritance will
    endure for ever.
In times of disaster they will not
    wither;
  in days of famine they will
    enjoy plenty.

But the wicked will perish:
  The LORD's enemies will be
    like the beauty of
    the fields,
  they will vanish—vanish like
    smoke.

The wicked borrow and do not
    repay,
  but the righteous give
    generously;
those the LORD blesses will inherit
    the land,
  but those he curses will be cut
    off.

If the LORD delights in a man's
way,
 he makes his steps firm;
though he stumble, he will not
 fall,
 for the LORD upholds him with
 his hand.

I was young and now I am old,
 yet I have never seen the
 righteous forsaken
 or their children begging bread.
They are always generous and
 lend freely;
 their children will be blessed.

Turn from evil and do good;
 then you will dwell in the land
 for ever.
For the LORD loves the just
 and will not forsake his faithful
 ones.

They will be protected for ever,
 but the offspring of the wicked
 will be cut off;
the righteous will inherit the land
 and dwell in it for ever.

The mouth of the righteous man
 utters wisdom,
 and his tongue speaks what is
 just.
The law of his God is in his
 heart;
 his feet do not slip.

The wicked lie in wait for the
 righteous,
 seeking their very lives;

but the LORD will not leave them
 in their power
 or let them be condemned when
 brought to trial.

Wait for the LORD
 and keep his way.
He will exalt you to inherit the land;
 when the wicked are cut off,
 you will see it.

I have seen a wicked and ruthless
 man
 flourishing like a green tree in
 its native soil,
but he soon passed away and was
 no more;
 though I looked for him, he
 could not be found.

Consider the blameless, observe
 the upright;
 there is a future for the man of
 peace.
But all sinners will be destroyed;
 the future of the wicked will be
 cut off.

The salvation of the righteous
 comes from the LORD;
 he is their stronghold in time of
 trouble.
The LORD helps them and delivers
 them;
 he delivers them from the
 wicked and saves them,
 because they take refuge in him.

✍

# Psalm 38

*A psalm of David. A petition.*

O LORD, do not rebuke me in your
anger
or discipline me in your wrath.
For your arrows have pierced me,
and your hand has come down
upon me.
Because of your wrath there is no
health in my body;
my bones have no soundness
because of my sin.
My guilt has overwhelmed me
like a burden too heavy to bear.

My wounds fester and are
loathsome
because of my sinful folly.
I am bowed down and brought
very low;
all day long I go about
mourning.
My back is filled with searing
pain;
there is no health in my body.
I am feeble and utterly crushed;
I groan in anguish of heart.

All my longings lie open before
you, O Lord:
my sighing is not hidden from
you.
My heart pounds, my strength
fails me;
even the light has gone from
my eyes.
My friends and companions avoid
me because of my wounds;
my neighbours stay far away.

Those who seek my life set their
traps,
those who would harm me talk
of my ruin;
all day long they plot deception.

I am like a deaf man, who cannot
hear,
like a mute, who cannot open
his mouth;
I have become like a man who
does not hear,
whose mouth can offer no
reply.
I wait for you, O LORD;
you will answer, O Lord my
God.
For I said, "Do not let them gloat
or exalt themselves over me
when my foot slips."

For I am about to fall,
and my pain is ever with me.
I confess my iniquity;
I am troubled by my sin.
Many are those who are my
vigorous enemies;
those who hate me without
reason are numerous.
Those who repay my good with
evil
slander me when I pursue what
is good.

O LORD, do not forsake me;
be not far from me, O my God.
Come quickly to help me,
O Lord my Saviour.

~

## Psalm 39

*For the director of music. For Jeduthun.*
*A psalm of David.*

I said, "I will watch my ways
and keep my tongue from sin;
I will put a muzzle on my mouth
as long as the wicked are in my
presence."
But when I was silent and still,
not even saying anything good,
my anguish increased.
My heart grew hot within me,
and as I meditated, the fire
burned;
then I spoke with my tongue:

"Show me, O LORD, my life's end
and the number of my days;
let me know how fleeting is my
life.
You have made my days a mere
handbreadth;
the span of my years is as
nothing before you.
Each man's life is but a breath.
*Selah*
Man is a mere phantom as he
goes to and fro:
He bustles about, but only in
vain;
he heaps up wealth, not
knowing who will get it.

"But now, Lord, what do I look for?
My hope is in you.
Save me from all my
transgressions;
do not make me the scorn of
fools.

I was silent; I would not open my
mouth,
for you are the one who has
done this.
Remove your scourge from me;
I am overcome by the blow of
your hand.
You rebuke and discipline men for
their sin;
you consume their wealth like a
moth—
each man is but a breath. *Selah*

"Hear my prayer, O LORD,
listen to my cry for help;
be not deaf to my weeping.
For I dwell with you as an alien,
a stranger, as all my fathers were.
Look away from me, that I may
rejoice again
before I depart and am no
more."

## Psalm 40

*For the director of music. Of David. A*
*psalm.*

I waited patiently for the LORD;
he turned to me and heard my cry.
He lifted me out of the slimy pit,
out of the mud and mire;
he set my feet on a rock
and gave me a firm place to
stand.
He put a new song in my mouth,
a hymn of praise to our God.
Many will see and fear
and put their trust in the LORD.

Blessed is the man
   who makes the LORD his trust,
who does not look to the proud,
   to those who turn aside to false
      gods.
Many, O LORD my God,
   are the wonders you have
      done.
The things you planned for us
   no-one can recount to you;
were I to speak and tell of them,
   they would be too many to
      declare.

Sacrifice and offering you did not
   desire,
   but my ears you have pierced;
burnt offerings and sin offerings
   you did not require.
Then I said, "Here I am, I have
      come—
   it is written about me in the
      scroll.
I desire to do your will, O my God;
   your law is within my heart."

I proclaim righteousness in the
      great assembly;
   I do not seal my lips,
   as you know, O LORD.
I do not hide your righteousness
      in my heart;
   I speak of your faithfulness and
      salvation.
I do not conceal your love and
      your truth
   from the great assembly.

Do not withhold your mercy from
   me, O LORD;

may your love and your truth
   always protect me.
For troubles without number
   surround me;
   my sins have overtaken me, and
      I cannot see.
They are more than the hairs of
      my head,
   and my heart fails within me.

Be pleased, O LORD, to save me;
   O LORD, come quickly to help me.
May all who seek to take my life
   be put to shame and confusion;
may all who desire my ruin
   be turned back in disgrace.
May those who say to me, "Aha!
      Aha!"
   be appalled at their own shame.
But may all who seek you
   rejoice and be glad in you;
may those who love your
      salvation always say,
   "The LORD be exalted!"

Yet I am poor and needy;
   may the Lord think of me.
You are my help and my
      deliverer;
   O my God, do not delay.

❧

## Psalm 41

*For the director of music. A psalm of David.*

Blessed is he who has regard for
   the weak;
   the LORD delivers him in times
   of trouble.

The LORD will protect him and
    preserve his life;
  he will bless him in the land
  and not surrender him to the
    desire of his foes.
The LORD will sustain him on his
    sick-bed
  and restore him from his bed of
    illness.

I said, "O LORD, have mercy on
    me;
  heal me, for I have sinned
    against you."
My enemies say of me in malice,
  "When will he die and his name
    perish?"
Whenever one comes to see me,
  he speaks falsely, while his
    heart gathers slander;
  then he goes out and spreads it
    abroad.

All my enemies whisper together
    against me;
  they imagine the worst for me,
    saying,
"A vile disease has beset him;
  he will never get up from the
    place where he lies."
Even my close friend, whom I
    trusted,
  he who shared my bread,
  has lifted up his heel against
    me.

But you, O LORD, have mercy on
    me;
  raise me up, that I may repay
    them.

I know that you are pleased with
    me,
  for my enemy does not triumph
    over me.
In my integrity you uphold me
  and set me in your presence for
    ever.

Praise be to the LORD, the God of
    Israel,
  from everlasting to everlasting.
    Amen and Amen.

# BOOK II (Psalms 42–72)

## Psalm 42

*For the director of music. A* maskil *of
the Sons of Korah.*

As the deer pants for streams of
    water,
  so my soul pants for you, O God.
My soul thirsts for God, for the
    living God.
  When can I go and meet with
    God?
My tears have been my food
  day and night,
while men say to me all day long,
  "Where is your God?"
These things I remember
  as I pour out my soul:
how I used to go with the
    multitude,
  leading the procession to the
    house of God,
with shouts of joy and
    thanksgiving
  among the festive throng.

Why are you downcast, O my
    soul?
  Why so disturbed within me?
Put your hope in God,
  for I will yet praise him,
  my Saviour and my God.

My soul is downcast within me;
  therefore I will remember you
from the land of the Jordan,
  the heights of Hermon—from
    Mount Mizar.
Deep calls to deep
  in the roar of your waterfalls;
all your waves and breakers
  have swept over me.

By day the LORD directs his love,
  at night his song is with me—
  a prayer to the God of my
    life.

I say to God my Rock,
  "Why have you forgotten me?
Why must I go about mourning,
  oppressed by the enemy?"
My bones suffer mortal agony
  as my foes taunt me,
saying to me all day long,
  "Where is your God?"

Why are you downcast, O my
    soul?
  Why so disturbed within me?
Put your hope in God,
  for I will yet praise him,
  my Saviour and my God.

## Psalm 43

Vindicate me, O God,
  and plead my cause against an
    ungodly nation;
  rescue me from deceitful and
    wicked men.
You are God my stronghold.
  Why have you rejected me?
Why must I go about mourning,
  oppressed by the enemy?
Send forth your light and your
    truth,
  let them guide me;
let them bring me to your holy
    mountain,
  to the place where you dwell.
Then will I go to the altar of God,
  to God, my joy and my delight.
I will praise you with the harp,
  O God, my God.

Why are you downcast, O my
    soul?
  Why so disturbed within me?
Put your hope in God,
  for I will yet praise him,
  my Saviour and my God.

## Psalm 44

*For the director of music. Of the Sons of
Korah. A maskil.*

We have heard with our ears, O
    God;
  our fathers have told us
what you did in their days,
  in days long ago.

With your hand you drove out
the nations
and planted our fathers;
you crushed the peoples
and made our fathers flourish.
It was not by their sword that
they won the land,
nor did their arm bring them
victory;
it was your right hand, your arm,
and the light of your face, for
you loved them.

You are my King and my God,
who decrees victories for Jacob.
Through you we push back our
enemies;
through your name we trample
our foes.
I do not trust in my bow,
my sword does not bring me
victory;
but you give us victory over our
enemies,
you put our adversaries to shame.
In God we make our boast all day
long,
and we will praise your name
for ever.                    *Selah*

But now you have rejected and
humbled us;
you no longer go out with our
armies.
You made us retreat before the
enemy,
and our adversaries have
plundered us.
You gave us up to be devoured
like sheep

and have scattered us among
the nations.
You sold your people for a
pittance,
gaining nothing from their sale.

You have made us a reproach to
our neighbours,
the scorn and derision of those
around us.
You have made us a byword
among the nations;
the peoples shake their heads at
us.
My disgrace is before me all day
long,
and my face is covered with
shame
at the taunts of those who
reproach and revile me,
because of the enemy, who is
bent on revenge.

All this happened to us,
though we had not forgotten
you
or been false to your covenant.
Our hearts had not turned back;
our feet had not strayed from
your path.
But you crushed us and made us
a haunt for jackals
and covered us over with deep
darkness.

If we had forgotten the name of
our God
or spread out our hands to a
foreign god,
would not God have discovered it,

since he knows the secrets of
the heart?
Yet for your sake we face death
all day long;
we are considered as sheep to
be slaughtered.

Awake, O Lord! Why do you
sleep?
Rouse yourself! Do not reject us
for ever.
Why do you hide your face
and forget our misery and
oppression?

We are brought down to the dust;
our bodies cling to the ground.
Rise up and help us;
redeem us because of your
unfailing love.

~

## Psalm 45

*For the director of music. To the tune
of "Lilies". Of the Sons of Korah. A
maskil. A wedding song.*

My heart is stirred by a noble
theme
as I recite my verses for the
king;
my tongue is the pen of a
skilful writer.

You are the most excellent of men
and your lips have been
anointed with grace,
since God has blessed you for
ever.

Gird your sword upon your side,
O mighty one;
clothe yourself with splendour
and majesty.
In your majesty ride forth
victoriously
on behalf of truth, humility and
righteousness;
let your right hand display
awesome deeds.
Let your sharp arrows pierce the
hearts of the king's enemies;
let the nations fall beneath your
feet.
Your throne, O God, will last for
ever and ever;
a sceptre of justice will be the
sceptre of your kingdom.
You love righteousness and hate
wickedness;
therefore God, your God, has
set you above your
companions
by anointing you with the oil of
joy.
All your robes are fragrant with
myrrh and aloes and cassia;
from palaces adorned with
ivory
the music of the strings makes
you glad.
Daughters of kings are among
your honoured women;
at your right hand is the royal
bride in gold of Ophir.

Listen, O daughter, consider and
give ear:
Forget your people and your
father's house.

The king is enthralled by your
beauty;
    honour him, for he is your lord.
The Daughter of Tyre will come
    with a gift,
    men of wealth will seek your
    favour.

All glorious is the princess within
    ˌher chamberˌ;
    her gown is interwoven with gold.
In embroidered garments she is
    led to the king;
    her virgin companions follow
    her
    and are brought to you.
They are led in with joy and
    gladness;
    they enter the palace of the
    king.

Your sons will take the place of
    your fathers;
    you will make them princes
    throughout the land.
I will perpetuate your memory
    through all generations;
    therefore the nations will praise
    you for ever and ever.

∽

## Psalm 46

*For the director of music. Of the Sons of
Korah. According to* alamoth. *A song.*

God is our refuge and strength,
    an ever-present help in trouble.
Therefore we will not fear, though
    the earth give way

and the mountains fall into the
    heart of the sea,
though its waters roar and foam
    and the mountains quake with
    their surging.          *Selah*

There is a river whose streams
    make glad the city of God,
    the holy place where the Most
    High dwells.
God is within her, she will not fall;
    God will help her at break of
    day.
Nations are in uproar, kingdoms
    fall;
    he lifts his voice, the earth melts.

The LORD Almighty is with us;
    the God of Jacob is our fortress.
                              *Selah*

Come and see the works of the LORD,
    the desolations he has brought
    on the earth.
He makes wars cease to the ends
    of the earth;
    he breaks the bow and shatters
    the spear,
    he burns the shields with fire.
"Be still, and know that I am God;
    I will be exalted among the
    nations,
    I will be exalted in the earth."

The LORD Almighty is with us;
    the God of Jacob is our fortress.
                              *Selah*

∽

## Psalm 47

*For the director of music. Of the Sons of Korah. A psalm.*

Clap your hands, all you nations;
  shout to God with cries of
    joy.
How awesome is the LORD Most
    High,
  the great King over all the
    earth!
He subdued nations under us,
  peoples under our feet.
He chose our inheritance for us,
  the pride of Jacob, whom he
    loved.                    *Selah*

God has ascended amid shouts of
    joy,
  the LORD amid the sounding of
    trumpets.
Sing praises to God, sing praises;
  sing praises to our King, sing
    praises.

For God is the King of all the
    earth;
  sing to him a psalm of praise.
God reigns over the nations;
  God is seated on his holy
    throne.
The nobles of the nations assemble
  as the people of the God of
    Abraham,
for the kings of the earth belong
    to God;
  he is greatly exalted.

## Psalm 48

*A song. A psalm of the Sons of Korah.*

Great is the LORD, and most
    worthy of praise,
  in the city of our God, his holy
    mountain.
It is beautiful in its loftiness,
  the joy of the whole earth.
Like the utmost heights of Zaphon
    is Mount Zion,
  the city of the Great King.
God is in her citadels;
  he has shown himself to be her
    fortress.

When the kings joined forces,
  when they advanced together,
they saw ˌherˌ and were astounded;
  they fled in terror.
Trembling seized them there,
  pain like that of a woman in
    labour.
You destroyed them like ships of
    Tarshish
  shattered by an east wind.

As we have heard,
  so have we seen
in the city of the LORD Almighty,
  in the city of our God:
  God makes her secure for ever.
                          *Selah*

Within your temple, O God,
  we meditate on your unfailing
    love.
Like your name, O God,
  your praise reaches to the ends
    of the earth;

41

your right hand is filled with
righteousness.
Mount Zion rejoices,
the villages of Judah are glad
because of your judgments.

Walk about Zion, go round her,
count her towers,
consider well her ramparts,
view her citadels,
that you may tell of them to the
next generation.
For this God is our God for ever
and ever;
he will be our guide even to the
end.

∾

## Psalm 49

*For the director of music. Of the Sons of
Korah. A psalm.*

Hear this, all you peoples;
listen, all who live in
this world,
both low and high,
rich and poor alike:
My mouth will speak words of
wisdom;
the utterance from my heart
will give understanding.
I will turn my ear to a proverb;
with the harp I will expound
my riddle:

Why should I fear when evil days
come,
when wicked deceivers
surround me—

those who trust in their wealth
and boast of their great riches?
No man can redeem the life of
another
or give to God a ransom for
him—
the ransom for a life is costly,
no payment is ever enough—
that he should live on for ever
and not see decay.

For all can see that wise men die;
the foolish and the senseless
alike perish
and leave their wealth to
others.
Their tombs will remain their
houses for ever,
their dwellings for endless
generations,
though they had named lands
after themselves.

But man, despite his riches, does
not endure;
he is like the beasts that perish.

This is the fate of those who trust
in themselves,
and of their followers, who
approve their sayings. *Selah*
Like sheep they are destined for
the grave,
and death will feed on them.
The upright will rule over them in
the morning;
their forms will decay in the
grave,
far from their princely
mansions.

But God will redeem my life from
    the grave;
  he will surely take me to
    himself.    *Selah*

Do not be overawed when a man
    grows rich,
  when the splendour of his
    house increases;
for he will take nothing with him
    when he dies,
  his splendour will not descend
    with him.
Though while he lived he counted
    himself blessed—
  and men praise you when you
    prosper—
he will join the generation of his
    fathers,
  who will never see the light ˏof
    lifeˌ.

A man who has riches without
    understanding
  is like the beasts that perish.

～

# Psalm 50
*A psalm of Asaph.*

The Mighty One, God, the LORD,
  speaks and summons the earth
  from the rising of the sun to the
    place where it sets.
From Zion, perfect in beauty,
  God shines forth.
Our God comes and will not be
    silent;
  a fire devours before him,

and around him a tempest
    rages.
He summons the heavens above,
  and the earth, that he may
    judge his people:
"Gather to me my consecrated
    ones,
  who made a covenant with me
    by sacrifice."
And the heavens proclaim his
    righteousness,
  for God himself is judge.    *Selah*

"Hear, O my people, and I will
    speak,
  O Israel, and I will testify
    against you:
  I am God, your God.
I do not rebuke you for your
    sacrifices
  or your burnt offerings, which
    are ever before me.
I have no need of a bull from
    your stall
  or of goats from your pens,
for every animal of the forest is
    mine,
  and the cattle on a thousand
    hills.
I know every bird in the
    mountains,
  and the creatures of the field
    are mine.
If I were hungry I would not tell
    you,
  for the world is mine, and all
    that is in it.
Do I eat the flesh of bulls
  or drink the blood of goats?
Sacrifice thank-offerings to God,

fulfil your vows to the Most
  High,
and call upon me in the day of
    trouble;
  I will deliver you, and you will
    honour me."

But to the wicked, God says:

"What right have you to recite my
    laws
  or take my covenant on your lips?
You hate my instruction
  and cast my words behind you.
When you see a thief, you join
    with him;
  you throw in your lot with
    adulterers.
You use your mouth for evil
  and harness your tongue to
    deceit.
You speak continually against
    your brother
  and slander your own mother's
    son.
These things you have done and I
    kept silent;
  you thought I was altogether
    like you.
But I will rebuke you
  and accuse you to your face.

"Consider this, you who forget God,
  or I will tear you to pieces, with
    none to rescue:
He who sacrifices thank-offerings
    honours me,
  and he prepares the way
  so that I may show him the
    salvation of God."

# Psalm 51

*For the director of music. A psalm of*
*David. When the prophet Nathan came*
*to him after David had committed*
*adultery with Bathsheba.*

Have mercy on me, O God,
  according to your unfailing
    love;
according to your great
        compassion
  blot out my transgressions.
Wash away all my iniquity
  and cleanse me from my sin.

For I know my transgressions,
  and my sin is always before
    me.
Against you, you only, have I
    sinned
  and done what is evil in your
    sight,
so that you are proved right when
    you speak
  and justified when you judge.
Surely I was sinful at birth,
  sinful from the time my mother
    conceived me.
Surely you desire truth in the
    inner parts;
  you teach me wisdom in the
    inmost place.

Cleanse me with hyssop, and I
    shall be clean;
  wash me, and I shall be whiter
    than snow.
Let me hear joy and gladness;
  let the bones you have crushed
    rejoice.

Hide your face from my sins
   and blot out all my iniquity.

Create in me a pure heart, O God,
   and renew a steadfast spirit
      within me.
Do not cast me from your
      presence
   or take your Holy Spirit from
      me.
Restore to me the joy of your
      salvation
   and grant me a willing spirit, to
      sustain me.

Then I will teach transgressors
      your ways,
   and sinners will turn back to
      you.
Save me from bloodguilt, O God,
   the God who saves me,
   and my tongue will sing of
      your righteousness.
O Lord, open my lips,
   and my mouth will declare
      your praise.
You do not delight in sacrifice, or
      I would bring it;
   you do not take pleasure in
      burnt offerings.
The sacrifices of God are a broken
      spirit;
   a broken and contrite heart,
   O God, you will not despise.

In your good pleasure make Zion
      prosper;
   build up the walls of Jerusalem.
Then there will be righteous
      sacrifices,

whole burnt offerings to delight
      you;
   then bulls will be offered on
      your altar.

≈

## Psalm 52

*For the director of music. A* maskil *of David. When Doeg the Edomite had gone to Saul and told him: "David has gone to the house of Ahimelech."*

Why do you boast of evil, you
      mighty man?
   Why do you boast all day long,
   you who are a disgrace in the
      eyes of God?
Your tongue plots destruction;
   it is like a sharpened razor,
   you who practise deceit.
You love evil rather than good,
   falsehood rather than speaking
      the truth.    *Selah*
You love every harmful word,
   O you deceitful tongue!

Surely God will bring you down
      to everlasting ruin:
   He will snatch you up and tear
      you from your tent;
   he will uproot you from the
      land of the living.   *Selah*
The righteous will see and fear;
   they will laugh at him, saying,
"Here now is the man
   who did not make God his
      stronghold
but trusted in his great wealth
   and grew strong by destroying
      others!"

But I am like an olive tree
  flourishing in the house of God;
I trust in God's unfailing love
  for ever and ever.
I will praise you for ever for what
  you have done;
  in your name I will hope, for
    your name is good.
  I will praise you in the presence
    of your saints.

∽

## Psalm 53

*For the director of music. According to*
mahalath. *A maskil of David.*

The fool says in his heart,
  "There is no God."
They are corrupt, and their ways
  are vile;
  there is no-one who does good.

God looks down from heaven
  on the sons of men
to see if there are any who
  understand,
  any who seek God.
Everyone has turned away,
  they have together become
  corrupt;
there is no-one who does good,
  not even one.

Will the evildoers never learn—
  those who devour my people as
  men eat bread
  and who do not call on God?
There they were, overwhelmed
  with dread,

where there was nothing to
  dread.
God scattered the bones of those
  who attacked you;
  you put them to shame, for God
  despised them.

Oh, that salvation for Israel would
  come out of Zion!
  When God restores the fortunes
  of his people,
  let Jacob rejoice and Israel be
  glad!

∽

## Psalm 54

*For the director of music. With stringed
instruments. A maskil of David. When
the Ziphites had gone to Saul and said,
"Is not David hiding among us?"*

Save me, O God, by your name;
  vindicate me by your might.
Hear my prayer, O God;
  listen to the words of my
  mouth.

Strangers are attacking me;
  ruthless men seek my life—
  men without regard for God.
           *Selah*

Surely God is my help;
  the Lord is the one who
  sustains me.

Let evil recoil on those who
  slander me;
  in your faithfulness destroy them.

I will sacrifice a freewill offering
to you;
I will praise your name,
O LORD,
for it is good.
For he has delivered me from all
my troubles,
and my eyes have looked in
triumph on my foes.

~

# Psalm 55
*For the director of music. With stringed
instruments. A* maskil *of David.*

Listen to my prayer, O God,
do not ignore my plea;
hear me and answer me.
My thoughts trouble me and I am
distraught
at the voice of the enemy,
at the stares of the wicked;
for they bring down suffering
upon me
and revile me in their anger.

My heart is in anguish within me;
the terrors of death assail me.
Fear and trembling have beset me;
horror has overwhelmed me.
I said, "Oh, that I had the wings
of a dove!
I would fly away and be at rest—
I would flee far away
and stay in the desert;       *Selah*
I would hurry to my place of
shelter,
far from the tempest and
storm."

Confuse the wicked, O Lord,
confound their speech,
for I see violence and strife in
the city.
Day and night they prowl about
on its walls;
malice and abuse are within it.
Destructive forces are at work in
the city;
threats and lies never leave its
streets.

If an enemy were insulting me,
I could endure it;
if a foe were raising himself
against me,
I could hide from him.
But it is you, a man like myself,
my companion, my close friend,
with whom I once enjoyed sweet
fellowship
as we walked with the throng
at the house of God.

Let death take my enemies by
surprise;
let them go down alive to the
grave,
for evil finds lodging among
them.

But I call to God,
and the LORD saves me.
Evening, morning and noon
I cry out in distress,
and he hears my voice.
He ransoms me unharmed
from the battle waged against
me,
even though many oppose me.

God, who is enthroned for ever,
  will hear them and afflict
    them—                           *Selah*
men who never change their ways
  and have no fear of God.

My companion attacks his friends;
  he violates his covenant.
His speech is smooth as butter,
  yet war is in his heart;
his words are more soothing than
    oil,
  yet they are drawn swords.

Cast your cares on the Lord
  and he will sustain you;
  he will never let the righteous fall.
But you, O God, will bring down
    the wicked
  into the pit of corruption;
bloodthirsty and deceitful men
  will not live out half their days.

But as for me, I trust in you.

~

## Psalm 56

*For the director of music. To the tune
of "A Dove on Distant Oaks". Of
David. A miktam. When the Phili-
stines had seized him in Gath.*

Be merciful to me, O God, for
    men hotly pursue me;
  all day long they press their attack.
My slanderers pursue me all day
    long;
  many are attacking me in their
    pride.

When I am afraid,
  I will trust in you.
In God, whose word I praise,
  in God I trust; I will not be
    afraid.
    What can mortal man do to
      me?

All day long they twist my words;
  they are always plotting to
    harm me.
They conspire, they lurk,
  they watch my steps,
  eager to take my life.

On no account let them escape;
  in your anger, O God, bring
    down the nations.
Record my lament;
  list my tears on your scroll—
  are they not in your record?

Then my enemies will turn back
  when I call for help.
  By this I will know that God is
    for me.
In God, whose word I praise,
  in the Lord, whose word I
    praise—
in God I trust; I will not be afraid.
  What can man do to me?

I am under vows to you, O God;
  I will present my thank-
    offerings to you.
For you have delivered me from
    death
  and my feet from stumbling,
that I may walk before God
  in the light of life.

## Psalm 57

*For the director of music. ⌐To the tune of⌐ "Do Not Destroy". Of David. A* miktam. *When he had fled from Saul into the cave.*

Have mercy on me, O God, have
mercy on me,
for in you my soul takes refuge.
I will take refuge in the shadow
of your wings
until the disaster has passed.

I cry out to God Most High,
to God, who fulfils ⌐his purpose⌐
for me.
He sends from heaven and saves
me,
rebuking those who hotly
pursue me;            *Selah*
God sends his love and his
faithfulness.

I am in the midst of lions;
I lie among ravenous beasts—
men whose teeth are spears and
arrows,
whose tongues are sharp
swords.

Be exalted, O God, above the
heavens;
let your glory be over all the
earth.

They spread a net for my feet—
I was bowed down in distress.
They dug a pit in my path—
but they have fallen into it
themselves.            *Selah*

My heart is steadfast, O God,
my heart is steadfast;
I will sing and make music.
Awake, my soul!
Awake, harp and lyre!
I will awaken the dawn.

I will praise you, O Lord, among
the nations;
I will sing of you among the
peoples.
For great is your love, reaching to
the heavens;
your faithfulness reaches to the
skies.

Be exalted, O God, above the
heavens;
let your glory be over all the
earth.

## Psalm 58

*For the director of music. ⌐To the tune of⌐ "Do Not Destroy". Of David. A* miktam.

Do you rulers indeed speak
justly?
Do you judge uprightly among
men?
No, in your heart you devise
injustice,
and your hands mete out
violence on the earth.
Even from birth the wicked go
astray;
from the womb they are
wayward and speak lies.

Their venom is like the venom of
    a snake,
  like that of a cobra that has
    stopped its ears,
that will not heed the tune of the
    charmer,
  however skilful the enchanter
    may be.

Break the teeth in their mouths, O
    God;
  tear out, O Lord, the fangs of
    the lions!
Let them vanish like water that
    flows away;
  when they draw the bow, let
    their arrows be blunted.
Like a slug melting away as it
    moves along,
  like a stillborn child, may they
    not see the sun.

Before your pots can feel ˎthe heat
    of˩ the thorns—
  whether they be green or dry—
    the wicked will be swept
    away.
The righteous will be glad when
    they are avenged,
  when they bathe their feet in
    the blood of the wicked.
Then men will say,
  "Surely the righteous still are
    rewarded;
  surely there is a God who
    judges the earth."

≈

# Psalm 59

*For the director of music. ˎTo the tune
of˩ "Do Not Destroy". Of David. A
miktam. When Saul had sent men to
watch David's house in order to kill
him.*

Deliver me from my enemies,
    O God;
  protect me from those who rise
    up against me.
Deliver me from evildoers
  and save me from bloodthirsty
    men.

See how they lie in wait for me!
  Fierce men conspire against me
for no offence or sin of mine,
    O Lord.
I have done no wrong, yet they
    are ready to attack me.
  Arise to help me; look on my
    plight!
O Lord God Almighty, the God of
    Israel,
  rouse yourself to punish all the
    nations;
  show no mercy to wicked
    traitors.      *Selah*

They return at evening,
  snarling like dogs,
  and prowl about the city.
See what they spew from their
    mouths—
  they spew out swords from
    their lips,
  and they say, "Who can hear us?"
But you, O Lord, laugh at them;
  you scoff at all those nations.

O my Strength, I watch for you;
   you, O God, are my fortress,
      my loving God.

God will go before me
   and will let me gloat over those
      who slander me.
But do not kill them, O Lord our
      shield,
   or my people will forget.
In your might make them wander
      about,
   and bring them down.
For the sins of their mouths,
   for the words of their lips,
   let them be caught in their
      pride.
For the curses and lies they utter,
   consume them in wrath,
   consume them till they are no
      more.
Then it will be known to the ends
      of the earth
   that God rules over Jacob.  *Selah*

They return at evening,
   snarling like dogs,
   and prowl about the city.
They wander about for food
   and howl if not satisfied.
But I will sing of your strength,
   in the morning I will sing of
      your love;
for you are my fortress,
   my refuge in times of trouble.

O my Strength, I sing praise to
      you;
   you, O God, are my fortress,
      my loving God.

## Psalm 60

*For the director of music. To the tune
of, "The Lily of the Covenant". A*
miktam *of David. For teaching. When
he fought Aram Naharaim and Aram
Zobah, and when Joab returned and
struck down twelve thousand Edomites
in the Valley of Salt.*

You have rejected us, O God, and
      burst forth upon us;
   you have been angry—now
      restore us!
You have shaken the land and
      torn it open;
   mend its fractures, for it is
      quaking.
You have shown your people
      desperate times;
   you have given us wine that
      makes us stagger.

But for those who fear you, you
      have raised a banner
   to be unfurled against the bow.
              *Selah*

Save us and help us with your
      right hand,
   that those you love may be
      delivered.
God has spoken from his
      sanctuary:
   "In triumph I will parcel out
      Shechem
   and measure off the Valley of
      Succoth.
Gilead is mine, and Manasseh is
      mine;
   Ephraim is my helmet,

Judah my sceptre.
Moab is my washbasin,
　upon Edom I toss my sandal;
　over Philistia I shout in
　　triumph."

Who will bring me to the fortified
　　city?
　Who will lead me to Edom?
Is it not you, O God, you who
　　have rejected us
　and no longer go out with our
　　armies?
Give us aid against the enemy,
　for the help of man
　is worthless.
With God we shall gain the
　　victory,
　and he will trample down our
　　enemies.

∾

# Psalm 61

*For the director of music. With stringed
instruments. Of David.*

Hear my cry, O God;
　listen to my prayer.

From the ends of the earth I call
　　to you,
　I call as my heart grows faint;
　lead me to the rock that is
　　higher than I.
For you have been my refuge,
　a strong tower against the foe.

I long to dwell in your tent for
　ever

and take refuge in the shelter of
　your wings.　　*Selah*
For you have heard my vows, O
　God;
　you have given me the heritage
　of those who fear your
　name.

Increase the days of the king's life,
　his years for many generations.
May he be enthroned in God's
　　presence for ever;
　appoint your love and
　　faithfulness to protect him.

Then will I ever sing praise to
　　your name
　and fulfil my vows day after
　day.

∾

# Psalm 62

*For the director of music. For Jeduthun.
A psalm of David.*

My soul finds rest in God alone;
　my salvation comes from him.
He alone is my rock and my
　　salvation;
　he is my fortress, I shall never
　be shaken.

How long will you assault a man?
　Would all of you throw him
　　down—
　this leaning wall, this tottering
　fence?
They fully intend to topple him
　from his lofty place;

they take delight in lies.
With their mouths they bless,
  but in their hearts they curse.
                              *Selah*


Find rest, O my soul, in God
  alone;
  my hope comes from him.
He alone is my rock and my
  salvation;
  he is my fortress, I shall not be
  shaken.
My salvation and my honour
  depend on God;
  he is my mighty rock, my refuge.
Trust in him at all times, O
  people;
  pour out your hearts to him,
  for God is our refuge.    *Selah*


Lowborn men are but a breath,
  the highborn are but a lie;
if weighed on a balance, they are
  nothing;
  together they are only a breath.
Do not trust in extortion
  or take pride in stolen goods;
though your riches increase,
  do not set your heart on them.


One thing God has spoken,
  two things have I heard:
that you, O God, are strong,
  and that you, O Lord, are
  loving.
Surely you will reward each
  person
  according to what he has done.

## Psalm 63

*A psalm of David. When he was in the
Desert of Judah.*


O God, you are my God,
  earnestly I seek you;
my soul thirsts for you,
  my body longs for you,
in a dry and weary land
  where there is no water.


I have seen you in the sanctuary
  and beheld your power and
  your glory.
Because your love is better than life,
  my lips will glorify you.
I will praise you as long as I live,
  and in your name I will lift up
  my hands.
My soul will be satisfied as with
  the richest of foods;
  with singing lips my mouth will
  praise you.


On my bed I remember you;
  I think of you through the
  watches of the night.
Because you are my help,
  I sing in the shadow of your
  wings.
My soul clings to you;
  your right hand upholds me.


They who seek my life will be
  destroyed;
  they will go down to the depths
  of the earth.
They will be given over to the
  sword
  and become food for jackals.

But the king will rejoice in God;
  all who swear by God's name
    will praise him,
  while the mouths of liars will
    be silenced.

∼

## Psalm 64

*For the director of music. A psalm of
David.*

Hear me, O God, as I voice my
    complaint;
  protect my life from the threat
    of the enemy.
Hide me from the conspiracy of
    the wicked,
  from that noisy crowd of
    evildoers.

They sharpen their tongues like
    swords
  and aim their words like deadly
    arrows.
They shoot from ambush at the
    innocent man;
  they shoot at him suddenly,
    without fear.

They encourage each other in evil
    plans,
  they talk about hiding their
    snares;
  they say, "Who will see them?"
They plot injustice and say,
  "We have devised a perfect
    plan!"
  Surely the mind and heart of
    man are cunning.

But God will shoot them with
    arrows;
  suddenly they will be struck
    down.
He will turn their own tongues
    against them
  and bring them to ruin;
  all who see them will shake
    their heads in scorn.

All mankind will fear;
  they will proclaim the works of
    God
  and ponder what he has done.
Let the righteous rejoice in the
    LORD
  and take refuge in him;
  let all the upright in heart
    praise him!

∼

## Psalm 65

*For the director of music. A psalm of
David. A song.*

Praise awaits you, O God, in Zion;
  to you our vows will be
    fulfilled.
O you who hear prayer,
  to you all men will come.
When we were overwhelmed by
    sins,
  you forgave our transgressions.
Blessed are those you choose
  and bring near to live in your
    courts!
We are filled with the good things
    of your house,
  of your holy temple.

You answer us with awesome
    deeds of righteousness,
    O God our Saviour,
the hope of all the ends of the
    earth
    and of the farthest seas,
who formed the mountains by
    your power,
    having armed yourself with
    strength,
who stilled the roaring of the
    seas,
    the roaring of their waves,
    and the turmoil of the
    nations.
Those living far away fear your
    wonders;
    where morning dawns and
    evening fades
    you call forth songs of joy.

You care for the land and water it;
    you enrich it abundantly.
The streams of God are filled with
    water
    to provide the people with
    corn,
    for so you have ordained it.
You drench its furrows
    and level its ridges;
you soften it with showers
    and bless its crops.
You crown the year with your
    bounty,
    and your carts overflow with
    abundance.
The grasslands of the desert
    overflow;
    the hills are clothed with
    gladness.

The meadows are covered with
    flocks
    and the valleys are mantled
    with corn;
    they shout for joy and sing.

~

## Psalm 66
*For the director of music. A song.
A psalm.*

Shout with joy to God, all the
    earth!
    Sing the glory of his name;
    make his praise glorious!
Say to God, "How awesome are
    your deeds!
    So great is your power
    that your enemies cringe before
    you.
All the earth bows down to you;
    they sing praise to you,
    they sing praise to your
    name."                    *Selah*

Come and see what God has
    done,
    how awesome his works on
    man's behalf!
He turned the sea into dry
    land,
    they passed through the waters
    on foot—
    come, let us rejoice in him.
He rules for ever by his power,
    his eyes watch the nations—
    let not the rebellious rise up
    against him.          *Selah*

Praise our God, O peoples,
  let the sound of his praise be
    heard;
he has preserved our lives
  and kept our feet from slipping.
For you, O God, tested us;
  you refined us like silver.
You brought us into prison
  and laid burdens on our backs.
You let men ride over our heads;
  we went through fire and water,
  but you brought us to a place
    of abundance.

I will come to your temple with
    burnt offerings
  and fulfil my vows to you—
vows my lips promised and my
    mouth spoke
  when I was in trouble.
I will sacrifice fat animals to you
  and an offering of rams;
  I will offer bulls and goats. *Selah*

Come and listen, all you who fear
    God;
  let me tell you what he has
    done for me.
I cried out to him with my mouth;
  his praise was on my tongue.
If I had cherished sin in my heart,
  the Lord would not have
    listened;
but God has surely listened
  and heard my voice in prayer.
Praise be to God,
  who has not rejected my prayer
  or withheld his love from me!

~

## Psalm 67

*For the director of music. With stringed
instruments. A psalm. A song.*

May God be gracious to us and
    bless us
  and make his face shine upon us,
                              *Selah*
that your ways may be known on
    earth,
  your salvation among all
    nations.

May the peoples praise you, O God;
  may all the peoples praise you.
May the nations be glad and sing
    for joy,
  for you rule the peoples justly
  and guide the nations of the
    earth.              *Selah*
May the peoples praise you, O God;
  may all the peoples praise you.

Then the land will yield its
    harvest,
  and God, our God, will bless us.
God will bless us,
  and all the ends of the earth
    will fear him.

~

## Psalm 68

*For the director of music. Of David. A
psalm. A song.*

May God arise, may his enemies
    be scattered;
  may his foes flee before him.

As smoke is blown away by the
wind,
  may you blow them away;
as wax melts before the fire,
  may the wicked perish before
    God.
But may the righteous be glad
  and rejoice before God;
  may they be happy and joyful.

Sing to God, sing praise to his
    name,
  extol him who rides on the
    clouds—
his name is the LORD—
  and rejoice before him.
A father to the fatherless, a
    defender of widows,
  is God in his holy dwelling.
God sets the lonely in families,
  he leads forth the prisoners
    with singing;
  but the rebellious live in a sun-
    scorched land.

When you went out before your
    people, O God,
  when you marched through the
    wasteland,       *Selah*
the earth shook,
  the heavens poured down rain,
before God, the One of Sinai,
  before God, the God of Israel.
You gave abundant showers,
    O God;
  you refreshed your weary
    inheritance.
Your people settled in it,
  and from your bounty, O God,
  you provided for the poor.

The Lord announced the word,
  and great was the company of
    those who proclaimed it:
"Kings and armies flee in haste;
  in the camps men divide the
    plunder.
Even while you sleep among the
    campfires,
  the wings of ˎmyˎ dove are
    sheathed with silver,
  its feathers with shining gold."
When the Almighty scattered the
    kings in the land,
  it was like snow fallen on
    Zalmon.

The mountains of Bashan are
    majestic mountains;
  rugged are the mountains of
    Bashan.
Why gaze in envy, O rugged
    mountains,
  at the mountain where God
    chooses to reign,
  where the LORD himself will
    dwell for ever?
The chariots of God are tens of
    thousands
  and thousands of thousands;
  the Lord ˎhas comeˎ from Sinai
    into his sanctuary.
When you ascended on high,
  you led captives in your train;
  you received gifts from men,
even from the rebellious—
  that you, O LORD God, might
    dwell there.

Praise be to the Lord, to God our
    Saviour,

who daily bears our burdens.
*Selah*
Our God is a God who saves;
from the Sovereign LORD comes
escape from death.

Surely God will crush the heads
of his enemies,
the hairy crowns of those who
go on in their sins.
The Lord says, "I will bring them
from Bashan;
I will bring them from the
depths of the sea,
that you may plunge your feet in
the blood of your foes,
while the tongues of your dogs
have their share."

Your procession has come into
view, O God,
the procession of my God and
King into the sanctuary.
In front are the singers, after them
the musicians;
with them are the maidens
playing tambourines.
Praise God in the great congregation;
praise the LORD in the assembly
of Israel.
There is the little tribe of
Benjamin, leading them,
there the great throng of
Judah's princes,
and there the princes of
Zebulun and of Naphtali.

Summon your power, O God;
show us your strength, O God,
as you have done before.

Because of your temple at
Jerusalem
kings will bring you gifts.
Rebuke the beast among the reeds,
the herd of bulls among the
calves of the nations.
Humbled, may it bring bars of
silver.
Scatter the nations who delight
in war.
Envoys will come from Egypt;
Cush will submit herself to
God.

Sing to God, O kingdoms of the
earth,
sing praise to the Lord,     *Selah*
to him who rides the ancient skies
above,
who thunders with mighty
voice.
Proclaim the power of God,
whose majesty is over Israel,
whose power is in the skies.
You are awesome, O God, in your
sanctuary;
the God of Israel gives power
and strength to his people.

Praise be to God!

≈

## Psalm 69

*For the director of music. To ˌthe tune
ofˌ "Lilies". Of David.*

Save me, O God,
for the waters have come up to
my neck.

I sink in the miry depths,
 where there is no foothold.
I have come into the deep waters;
 the floods engulf me.
I am worn out calling for help;
 my throat is parched.
My eyes fail,
 looking for my God.
Those who hate me without
   reason
 outnumber the hairs of my
   head;
many are my enemies without
   cause,
 those who seek to destroy me.
I am forced to restore
 what I did not steal.

You know my folly, O God;
 my guilt is not hidden from
   you.

May those who hope in you
 not be disgraced because of me,
 O Lord, the LORD Almighty;
may those who seek you
 not be put to shame because of
   me,
 O God of Israel.
For I endure scorn for your sake,
 and shame covers my face.
I am a stranger to my brothers,
 an alien to my own mother's
   sons;
for zeal for your house consumes
   me,
 and the insults of those who
   insult you fall on me.
When I weep and fast,
 I must endure scorn;

when I put on sackcloth,
 people make sport of me.
Those who sit at the gate mock
   me,
 and I am the song of the
   drunkards.

But I pray to you, O LORD,
 in the time of your favour;
in your great love, O God,
 answer me with your sure
   salvation.
Rescue me from the mire,
 do not let me sink;
deliver me from those who hate
   me,
 from the deep waters.
Do not let the floodwaters engulf
   me
 or the depths swallow me up
 or the pit close its mouth over
   me.
Answer me, O LORD, out of the
   goodness of your love;
 in your great mercy turn to me.
Do not hide your face from your
   servant;
 answer me quickly, for I am in
   trouble.
Come near and rescue me;
 redeem me because of my foes.

You know how I am scorned,
 disgraced and shamed;
 all my enemies are before you.
Scorn has broken my heart
 and has left me helpless;
I looked for sympathy, but there
   was none,
 for comforters, but I found none.

They put gall in my food
  and gave me vinegar for my
    thirst.

May the table set before them
    become a snare;
  may it become retribution and a
    trap.
May their eyes be darkened so
    that they cannot see,
  and their backs be bent for
    ever.
Pour out your wrath on them;
  let your fierce anger overtake
    them.
May their place be deserted;
  let there be no-one to dwell in
    their tents.
For they persecute those you
    wound
  and talk about the pain of those
    you hurt.
Charge them with crime upon
    crime;
  do not let them share in your
    salvation.
May they be blotted out of the
    book of life
  and not be listed with the
    righteous.

I am in pain and distress;
  may your salvation, O God,
    protect me.

I will praise God's name in song
  and glorify him with
    thanksgiving.
This will please the LORD more
    than an ox,

more than a bull with its horns
    and hoofs.
The poor will see and be glad—
  you who seek God, may your
    hearts live!
The LORD hears the needy
  and does not despise his captive
    people.

Let heaven and earth praise him,
  the seas and all that move in
    them,
for God will save Zion
  and rebuild the cities of Judah.
Then people will settle there and
    possess it;
  the children of his servants will
    inherit it,
  and those who love his name
    will dwell there.

≈

## Psalm 70

*For the director of music. Of David.*
*A petition.*

Hasten, O God, to save me;
  O LORD, come quickly to help
    me.
May those who seek my life
  be put to shame and confusion;
may all who desire my ruin
  be turned back in disgrace.
May those who say to me, "Aha!
    Aha!"
  turn back because of their
    shame.
But may all who seek you
  rejoice and be glad in you;

may those who love your
    salvation always say,
"Let God be exalted!"

Yet I am poor and needy;
    come quickly to me, O God.
You are my help and my
        deliverer;
    O LORD, do not delay.

~

## Psalm 71

In you, O LORD, I have taken
        refuge;
    let me never be put to shame.
Rescue me and deliver me in your
        righteousness;
    turn your ear to me and save me.
Be my rock of refuge,
    to which I can always go;
give the command to save me,
    for you are my rock and my
        fortress.
Deliver me, O my God, from the
        hand of the wicked,
    from the grasp of evil and cruel
        men.

For you have been my hope, O
        Sovereign LORD,
    my confidence since my youth.
From my birth I have relied on
        you;
    you brought me forth from my
        mother's womb.
    I will ever praise you.
I have become like a portent to
        many,

but you are my strong refuge.
My mouth is filled with your
        praise,
    declaring your splendour all
        day long.

Do not cast me away when I am
        old;
    do not forsake me when my
        strength is gone.
For my enemies speak against me;
    those who wait to kill me
        conspire together.
They say, "God has forsaken him;
    pursue him and seize him,
    for no-one will rescue him."
Be not far from me, O God;
    come quickly, O my God, to
        help me.
May my accusers perish in shame;
    may those who want to harm
        me
    be covered with scorn and
        disgrace.

But as for me, I shall always have
        hope;
    I will praise you more and
        more.
My mouth will tell of your
        righteousness,
    of your salvation all day long,
    though I know not its measure.
I will come and proclaim your
        mighty acts, O Sovereign
        LORD;
    I will proclaim your
        righteousness, yours alone.
Since my youth, O God, you have
        taught me,

and to this day I declare your
   marvellous deeds.
Even when I am old and grey,
   do not forsake me, O God,
till I declare your power to the
   next generation,
   your might to all who are to
      come.

Your righteousness reaches to the
   skies, O God,
   you who have done great
      things.
   Who, O God, is like you?
Though you have made me see
      troubles, many and bitter,
   you will restore my life again;
from the depths of the earth
   you will again bring me up.
You will increase my honour
   and comfort me once again.

I will praise you with the harp
   for your faithfulness, O my
      God;
I will sing praise to you with the
      lyre,
   O Holy One of Israel.
My lips will shout for joy
   when I sing praise to you—
   I, whom you have redeemed.
My tongue will tell of your
      righteous acts
   all day long,
for those who wanted to harm me
   have been put to shame and
      confusion.

∾

# Psalm 72
*Of Solomon.*

Endow the king with your justice,
   O God,
   the royal son with your
      righteousness.
He will judge your people in
      righteousness,
   your afflicted ones with justice.
The mountains will bring
      prosperity to the people,
   the hills the fruit of
      righteousness.
He will defend the afflicted
      among the people
   and save the children of the
      needy;
   he will crush the oppressor.

He will endure as long as the sun,
   as long as the moon, through all
      generations.
He will be like rain falling on a
      mown field,
   like showers watering the earth.
In his days the righteous will
      flourish;
   prosperity will abound till the
      moon is no more.

He will rule from sea to sea
   and from the River to the ends
      of the earth.
The desert tribes will bow before
      him
   and his enemies will lick the
      dust.
The kings of Tarshish and of
      distant shores

will bring tribute to him;
the kings of Sheba and Seba
    will present him gifts.
All kings will bow down to him
    and all nations will serve him.

For he will deliver the needy who
        cry out,
    the afflicted who have no-one to
        help.
He will take pity on the weak and
        the needy
    and save the needy from death.
He will rescue them from
        oppression and violence,
    for precious is their blood in his
        sight.

Long may he live!
    May gold from Sheba be given
        to him.
May people ever pray for him
    and bless him all day long.
Let corn abound throughout the
        land;
    on the tops of the hills may it
        sway.
Let its fruit flourish like Lebanon;
    let it thrive like the grass of the
        field.
May his name endure for ever;
    may it continue as long as the
        sun.

All nations will be blessed
        through him,
    and they will call him blessed.

Praise be to the LORD God, the
        God of Israel,

who alone does marvellous
        deeds.
Praise be to his glorious name for
        ever;
    may the whole earth be filled
        with his glory.
            Amen and Amen.

This concludes the prayers of
        David son of Jesse.


# BOOK III (Psalms 73–89)

## Psalm 73
*A psalm of Asaph.*

Surely God is good to Israel,
    to those who are pure in heart.

But as for me, my feet had almost
        slipped;
    I had nearly lost my foothold.
For I envied the arrogant
    when I saw the prosperity of
        the wicked.

They have no struggles;
    their bodies are healthy and
        strong.
They are free from the burdens
        common to man;
    they are not plagued by human
        ills.
Therefore pride is their necklace;
    they clothe themselves with
        violence.
From their callous hearts comes
        iniquity;

the evil conceits of their minds
know no limits.
They scoff, and speak with malice;
in their arrogance they threaten
oppression.
Their mouths lay claim to heaven,
and their tongues take
possession of the earth.
Therefore their people turn to
them
and drink up waters in
abundance.
They say, "How can God know?
Does the Most High have
knowledge?"

This is what the wicked are like—
always carefree, they increase in
wealth.

Surely in vain have I kept my
heart pure;
in vain have I washed my
hands in innocence.
All day long I have been plagued;
I have been punished every
morning.

If I had said, "I will speak thus,"
I would have betrayed your
children.
When I tried to understand all
this,
it was oppressive to me
till I entered the sanctuary of God;
then I understood their final
destiny.

Surely you place them on slippery
ground;

you cast them down to ruin.
How suddenly are they destroyed,
completely swept away by
terrors!
As a dream when one awakes,
so when you arise, O Lord,
you will despise them as
fantasies.

When my heart was grieved
and my spirit embittered,
I was senseless and ignorant;
I was a brute beast before you.

Yet I am always with you;
you hold me by my right
hand.
You guide me with your counsel,
and afterwards you will take
me into glory.
Whom have I in heaven but you?
And earth has nothing I desire
besides you.
My flesh and my heart may fail,
but God is the strength of my
heart
and my portion for ever.

Those who are far from you will
perish;
you destroy all who are
unfaithful to you.
But as for me, it is good to be
near God.
I have made the Sovereign LORD
my refuge;
I will tell of all your deeds.

## Psalm 74
*A maskil of Asaph.*

Why have you rejected us for
 ever, O God?
 Why does your anger smoulder
  against the sheep of your
  pasture?
Remember the people you
  purchased of old,
 the tribe of your inheritance,
  whom you redeemed—
 Mount Zion, where you
  dwelt.
Turn your steps towards these
  everlasting ruins,
 all this destruction the enemy
  has brought on the
  sanctuary.

Your foes roared in the place
  where you met with us;
 they set up their standards as
  signs.
They behaved like men wielding
  axes
 to cut through a thicket of
  trees.
They smashed all the carved
  panelling
 with their axes and hatchets.
They burned your sanctuary to
  the ground;
 they defiled the dwelling-place
  of your Name.
They said in their hearts, "We will
  crush them completely!"
 They burned every place where
  God was worshipped in the
  land.

We are given no miraculous signs;
 no prophets are left,
 and none of us knows how long
  this will be.

How long will the enemy mock
  you, O God?
 Will the foe revile your name
  for ever?
Why do you hold back your
  hand, your right hand?
 Take it from the folds of your
  garment and destroy them!

But you, O God, are my king
  from of old;
 you bring salvation upon the
  earth.
It was you who split open the sea
  by your power;
 you broke the heads of the
  monster in the waters.
It was you who crushed the heads
  of Leviathan
 and gave him as food to the
  creatures of the desert.
It was you who opened up
  springs and streams;
 you dried up the ever-flowing
  rivers.
The day is yours, and yours also
  the night;
 you established the sun and moon.
It was you who set all the
  boundaries of the earth;
 you made both summer and
  winter.

Remember how the enemy has
  mocked you, O LORD,

how foolish people have reviled
your name.
Do not hand over the life of your
dove to wild beasts;
do not forget the lives of
your afflicted people for
ever.
Have regard for your covenant,
because haunts of violence
fill the dark places of the
land.
Do not let the oppressed retreat in
disgrace;
may the poor and needy praise
your name.

Rise up, O God, and defend your
cause;
remember how fools mock you
all day long.
Do not ignore the clamour of your
adversaries,
the uproar of your enemies,
which rises continually.

∼

## Psalm 75

*For the director of music. To the tune
of "Do Not Destroy". A psalm of
Asaph. A song.*

We give thanks to you, O God,
we give thanks, for your Name
is near;
men tell of your wonderful
deeds.

You say, "I choose the appointed
time;

it is I who judge uprightly.
When the earth and all its people
quake,
it is I who hold its pillars firm.
*Selah*
To the arrogant I say, 'Boast no
more,'
and to the wicked, 'Do not lift
up your horns.
Do not lift your horns against
heaven;
do not speak with outstretched
neck.' "

No-one from the east or the west
or from the desert can exalt a
man.
But it is God who judges:
He brings one down, he exalts
another.
In the hand of the Lord is a cup
full of foaming wine mixed
with spices;
he pours it out, and all the wicked
of the earth
drink it down to its very
dregs.

As for me, I will declare this for
ever;
I will sing praise to the God of
Jacob.
I will cut off the horns of all the
wicked,
but the horns of the righteous
shall be lifted up.

∼

# Psalm 76

*For the director of music. With stringed
instruments. A psalm of Asaph.
A song.*

In Judah God is known;
  his name is great in Israel.
His tent is in Salem,
  his dwelling-place in Zion.
There he broke the flashing
    arrows,
  the shields and the swords, the
    weapons of war.          *Selah*

You are resplendent with light,
  more majestic than mountains
    rich with game.
Valiant men lie plundered,
  they sleep their last sleep;
not one of the warriors
  can lift his hands.
At your rebuke, O God of Jacob,
  both horse and chariot lie still.
You alone are to be feared.
  Who can stand before you
    when you are angry?
From heaven you pronounced
    judgment,
  and the land feared and was
    quiet—
when you, O God, rose up to judge,
  to save all the afflicted of the
    land.          *Selah*
Surely your wrath against men
    brings you praise,
  and the survivors of your wrath
    are restrained.

Make vows to the LORD your God
  and fulfil them;

let all the neighbouring lands
  bring gifts to the One to be
    feared.
He breaks the spirit of rulers;
  he is feared by the kings of the
    earth.

~

# Psalm 77

*For the director of music. For Jeduthun.
Of Asaph. A psalm.*

I cried out to God for help;
  I cried out to God to hear me.
When I was in distress, I sought
    the Lord;
  at night I stretched out untiring
    hands
  and my soul refused to be
    comforted.

I remembered you, O God, and I
    groaned;
  I mused, and my spirit grew
    faint.          *Selah*
You kept my eyes from closing;
  I was too troubled to speak.
I thought about the former days,
  the years of long ago;
I remembered my songs in the
    night.
  My heart mused and my spirit
    enquired:

"Will the Lord reject for ever?
  Will he never show his favour
    again?
Has his unfailing love vanished
  for ever?

Has his promise failed for all
time?
Has God forgotten to be merciful?
Has he in anger withheld his
compassion?" *Selah*

Then I thought, "To this I will
appeal:
the years of the right hand of
the Most High."
I will remember the deeds of the
LORD;
yes, I will remember your
miracles of long ago.
I will meditate on all your works
and consider all your mighty
deeds.

Your ways, O God, are holy.
What god is so great as our
God?
You are the God who performs
miracles;
you display your power among
the peoples.
With your mighty arm you
redeemed your people,
the descendants of Jacob and
Joseph. *Selah*

The waters saw you, O God,
the waters saw you and
writhed;
the very depths were
convulsed.
The clouds poured down water,
the skies resounded with
thunder;
your arrows flashed back and
forth.

Your thunder was heard in the
whirlwind,
your lightning lit up the world;
the earth trembled and quaked.
Your path led through the sea,
your way through the mighty
waters,
though your footprints were not
seen.

You led your people like a flock
by the hand of Moses and
Aaron.

∾

## Psalm 78
*A maskil of Asaph.*

O my people, hear my teaching;
listen to the words of my
mouth.
I will open my mouth in parables,
I will utter hidden things,
things from of old—
what we have heard and known,
what our fathers have told us.
We will not hide them from their
children;
we will tell the next generation
the praiseworthy deeds of the
LORD,
his power, and the wonders he
has done.
He decreed statutes for Jacob
and established the law in
Israel,
which he commanded our
forefathers
to teach their children,

so that the next generation would
know them,
even the children yet to be
born,
and they in turn would tell
their children.
Then they would put their trust in
God
and would not forget his deeds
but would keep his commands.
They would not be like their
forefathers—
a stubborn and rebellious
generation,
whose hearts were not loyal to
God,
whose spirits were not faithful
to him.

The men of Ephraim, though
armed with bows,
turned back on the day of
battle;
they did not keep God's covenant
and refused to live by his law.
They forgot what he had done,
the wonders he had shown
them.
He did miracles in the sight of
their fathers
in the land of Egypt, in the
region of Zoan.
He divided the sea and led them
through;
he made the water stand firm
like a wall.
He guided them with the cloud
by day
and with light from the fire all
night.

He split the rocks in the desert
and gave them water as
abundant as the seas;
he brought streams out of a rocky
crag
and made water flow down like
rivers.

But they continued to sin against
him,
rebelling in the desert against
the Most High.
They wilfully put God to the test
by demanding the food they
craved.
They spoke against God, saying,
"Can God spread a table in the
desert?
When he struck the rock, water
gushed out,
and streams flowed abundantly.
But can he also give us food?
Can he supply meat for his
people?"
When the LORD heard them, he
was very angry;
his fire broke out against Jacob,
and his wrath rose against
Israel,
for they did not believe in God
or trust in his deliverance.
Yet he gave a command to the
skies above
and opened the doors of the
heavens;
he rained down manna for the
people to eat,
he gave them the grain of
heaven.
Men ate the bread of angels;

he sent them all the food they
could eat.
He let loose the east wind from
the heavens
and led forth the south wind by
his power.
He rained meat down on them
like dust,
flying birds like sand on the
seashore.
He made them come down inside
their camp,
all around their tents.
They ate till they had more than
enough,
for he had given them what
they craved.
But before they turned from the
food they craved,
even while it was still in their
mouths,
God's anger rose against them;
he put to death the sturdiest
among them,
cutting down the young men of
Israel.

In spite of all this, they kept on
sinning;
in spite of his wonders, they
did not believe.
So he ended their days in futility
and their years in terror.
Whenever God slew them, they
would seek him;
they eagerly turned to him again.
They remembered that God was
their Rock,
that God Most High was their
Redeemer.

But then they would flatter him
with their mouths,
lying to him with their tongues;
their hearts were not loyal to him,
they were not faithful to his
covenant.
Yet he was merciful;
he forgave their iniquities
and did not destroy them.
Time after time he restrained his
anger
and did not stir up his full
wrath.
He remembered that they were
but flesh,
a passing breeze that does not
return.

How often they rebelled against
him in the desert
and grieved him in the
wasteland!
Again and again they put God to
the test;
they vexed the Holy One of
Israel.
They did not remember his
power—
the day he redeemed them from
the oppressor,
the day he displayed his
miraculous signs in Egypt,
his wonders in the region of
Zoan.
He turned their rivers to blood;
they could not drink from their
streams.
He sent swarms of flies that
devoured them,
and frogs that devastated them.

He gave their crops to the
  grasshopper,
    their produce to the locust.
He destroyed their vines with hail
  and their sycamore-figs with sleet.
He gave over their cattle to the
  hail,
    their livestock to bolts of
    lightning.
He unleashed against them his hot
  anger,
    his wrath, indignation and
    hostility—
a band of destroying angels.
He prepared a path for his anger;
  he did not spare them from
  death
    but gave them over to the
    plague.
He struck down all the firstborn
  of Egypt,
    the firstfruits of manhood in the
    tents of Ham.
But he brought his people out like
  a flock;
    he led them like sheep through
    the desert.
He guided them safely, so they
  were unafraid;
    but the sea engulfed their
    enemies.
Thus he brought them to the
  border of his holy land,
    to the hill country his right
    hand had taken.
He drove out nations before them
  and allotted their lands to them
    as an inheritance;
  he settled the tribes of Israel in
    their homes.

But they put God to the test
  and rebelled against the Most
  High;
    they did not keep his statutes.
Like their fathers they were
  disloyal and faithless,
    as unreliable as a faulty bow.
They angered him with their high
  places;
    they aroused his jealousy with
    their idols.
When God heard them, he was
  very angry;
    he rejected Israel completely.
He abandoned the tabernacle of
  Shiloh,
    the tent he had set up among
    men.
He sent ⸤the ark of⸥ his might into
  captivity,
    his splendour into the hands of
    the enemy.
He gave his people over to the
  sword;
    he was very angry with his
    inheritance.
Fire consumed their young men,
  and their maidens had no
    wedding songs;
their priests were put to the
  sword,
    and their widows could not weep.

Then the Lord awoke as from
  sleep,
    as a man wakes from the stupor
    of wine.
He beat back his enemies;
  he put them to everlasting
    shame.

Then he rejected the tents of
Joseph,
he did not choose the tribe of
Ephraim;
but he chose the tribe of Judah,
Mount Zion, which he loved.
He built his sanctuary like the
heights,
like the earth that he established
for ever.
He chose David his servant
and took him from the sheep
pens;
from tending the sheep he
brought him
to be the shepherd of his people
Jacob,
of Israel his inheritance.
And David shepherded them with
integrity of heart;
with skilful hands he led them.

∼

## Psalm 79
*A psalm of Asaph.*

O God, the nations have invaded
your inheritance;
they have defiled your holy
temple,
they have reduced Jerusalem to
rubble.
They have given the dead bodies
of your servants
as food to the birds of the air,
the flesh of your saints to the
beasts of the earth.
They have poured out blood like
water

all around Jerusalem,
and there is no-one to bury the
dead.
We are objects of reproach to our
neighbours,
of scorn and derision to those
around us.

How long, O LORD? Will you be
angry for ever?
How long will your jealousy
burn like fire?
Pour out your wrath on the
nations
that do not acknowledge you,
on the kingdoms
that do not call on your name;
for they have devoured Jacob
and destroyed his homeland.
Do not hold against us the sins of
the fathers;
may your mercy come quickly
to meet us,
for we are in desperate need.

Help us, O God our Saviour,
for the glory of your name;
deliver us and forgive our sins
for your name's sake.
Why should the nations say,
"Where is their God?"
Before our eyes, make known
among the nations
that you avenge the outpoured
blood of your servants.
May the groans of the prisoners
come before you;
by the strength of your arm
preserve those condemned to
die.

Pay back into the laps of our
    neighbours seven times
  the reproach they have hurled
    at you, O Lord.
Then we your people, the sheep of
    your pasture,
  will praise you for ever;
from generation to generation
  we will recount your praise.

&#126;

## Psalm 80

*For the director of music. To ˌthe tune*
*ofˌ "The Lilies of the Covenant".*
*Of Asaph. A psalm.*

Hear us, O Shepherd of Israel,
  you who lead Joseph like a
    flock;
you who sit enthroned between
    the cherubim, shine forth
  before Ephraim, Benjamin and
    Manasseh.
Awaken your might;
  come and save us.

Restore us, O God;
  make your face shine upon us,
  that we may be saved.

O Lord God Almighty,
  how long will your anger
    smoulder
  against the prayers of your
    people?
You have fed them with the bread
    of tears;
  you have made them drink
    tears by the bowlful.

You have made us a source of
    contention to our
    neighbours,
  and our enemies mock us.

Restore us, O God Almighty;
  make your face shine upon us,
  that we may be saved.

You brought a vine out of Egypt;
  you drove out the nations and
    planted it.
You cleared the ground for it,
  and it took root and filled the
    land.
The mountains were covered with
    its shade,
  the mighty cedars with its
    branches.
It sent out its boughs to the Sea,
  its shoots as far as the River.

Why have you broken down its
    walls
  so that all who pass by pick its
    grapes?
Boars from the forest ravage it
  and the creatures of the field
    feed on it.
Return to us, O God Almighty!
  Look down from heaven and
    see!
Watch over this vine,
  the root your right hand has
    planted,
  the son you have raised up for
    yourself.

Your vine is cut down, it is
  burned with fire;

at your rebuke your people
perish.
Let your hand rest on the man at
your right hand,
the son of man you have raised
up for yourself.
Then we will not turn away from
you;
revive us, and we will call on
your name.

Restore us, O LORD God Almighty;
make your face shine upon us,
that we may be saved.

~

# Psalm 81
*For the director of music. According to*
gittith. *Of Asaph.*

Sing for joy to God our strength;
shout aloud to the God of
Jacob!
Begin the music, strike the
tambourine,
play the melodious harp and
lyre.

Sound the ram's horn at the New
Moon,
and when the moon is full, on
the day of our Feast;
this is a decree for Israel,
an ordinance of the God of
Jacob.
He established it as a statute for
Joseph
when he went out against
Egypt,

where we heard a language we
did not understand.

He says, "I removed the burden
from their shoulders;
their hands were set free from
the basket.
In your distress you called and I
rescued you,
I answered you out of a
thundercloud;
I tested you at the waters of
Meribah.               *Selah*

"Hear, O my people, and I will
warn you—
if you would but listen to me,
O Israel!
You shall have no foreign god
among you;
you shall not bow down to an
alien god.
I am the LORD your God,
who brought you up out of
Egypt.
Open wide your mouth and I
will fill it.

"But my people would not listen
to me;
Israel would not submit to me.
So I gave them over to their
stubborn hearts
to follow their own devices.

"If my people would but listen to
me,
if Israel would follow my ways,
how quickly would I subdue their
enemies

and turn my hand against their
   foes!
Those who hate the LORD would
   cringe before him,
   and their punishment would
     last for ever.
But you would be fed with the
   finest of wheat;
   with honey from the rock I
     would satisfy you."

## Psalm 82
*A psalm of Asaph.*

God presides in the great assembly;
   he gives judgment among the
     "gods":

"How long will you defend the
   unjust
   and show partiality to the wicked?
              *Selah*
Defend the cause of the weak and
   fatherless;
   maintain the rights of the poor
     and oppressed.
Rescue the weak and needy;
   deliver them from the hand of
     the wicked.

"They know nothing, they
   understand nothing.
   They walk about in darkness;
   all the foundations of the earth
     are shaken.

"I said, 'You are "gods";
   you are all sons of the Most High.'

But you will die like mere men;
   you will fall like every other
     ruler."

Rise up, O God, judge the earth,
   for all the nations are your
     inheritance.

## Psalm 83
*A song. A psalm of Asaph.*

O God, do not keep silent;
   be not quiet, O God, be not
     still.
See how your enemies are astir,
   how your foes rear their heads.
With cunning they conspire
       against your people;
   they plot against those you
     cherish.
"Come," they say, "let us destroy
     them as a nation,
   that the name of Israel be
     remembered no more."

With one mind they plot
   together;
   they form an alliance against
     you—
the tents of Edom and the
     Ishmaelites,
   of Moab and the Hagrites,
Gebal, Ammon and Amalek,
   Philistia, with the people of
     Tyre.
Even Assyria has joined them
   to lend strength to the
        descendants of Lot.   *Selah*

Do to them as you did to
Midian,
as you did to Sisera and Jabin
at the river Kishon,
who perished at Endor
and became like refuse on the
ground.
Make their nobles like Oreb and
Zeeb,
all their princes like Zebah and
Zalmunna,
who said, "Let us take possession
of the pasture-lands of God."

Make them like tumble-weed,
O my God,
like chaff before the wind.
As fire consumes the forest
or a flame sets the mountains
ablaze,
so pursue them with your
tempest
and terrify them with your
storm.
Cover their faces with shame
so that men will seek your
name, O LORD.

May they ever be ashamed and
dismayed;
may they perish in disgrace.
Let them know that you, whose
name is the LORD—
that you alone are the Most
High over all the earth.

∿

## Psalm 84

*For the director of music. According to
gittith. Of the Sons of Korah. A psalm.*

How lovely is your dwelling-
place,
O LORD Almighty!
My soul yearns, even faints,
for the courts of the LORD;
my heart and my flesh cry out
for the living God.

Even the sparrow has found a
home,
and the swallow a nest for
herself,
where she may have her
young—
a place near your altar,
O LORD Almighty, my King and
my God.
Blessed are those who dwell in
your house;
they are ever praising you. *Selah*

Blessed are those whose strength
is in you,
who have set their hearts on
pilgrimage.
As they pass through the Valley
of Baca,
they make it a place of springs;
the autumn rains also cover it
with pools.
They go from strength to strength,
till each appears before God in
Zion.

Hear my prayer, O LORD God
Almighty;

listen to me, O God of Jacob.
*Selah*
Look upon our shield, O God;
  look with favour on your
    anointed one.

Better is one day in your courts
  than a thousand elsewhere;
I would rather be a doorkeeper in
    the house of my God
  than dwell in the tents of the
    wicked.
For the LORD God is a sun and
    shield;
  the LORD bestows favour and
    honour;
no good thing does he withhold
  from those whose walk is
    blameless.

O LORD Almighty,
  blessed is the man who trusts in
    you.

～

## Psalm 85

*For the director of music. Of the Sons of
Korah. A psalm.*

You showed favour to your land,
    O LORD;
  you restored the fortunes of
    Jacob.
You forgave the iniquity of your
    people
  and covered all their sins. *Selah*
You set aside all your wrath
  and turned from your fierce
    anger.

Restore us again, O God our Saviour,
  and put away your displeasure
    towards us.
Will you be angry with us for
    ever?
  Will you prolong your anger
    through all generations?
Will you not revive us again,
  that your people may rejoice in
    you?
Show us your unfailing love, O
    LORD,
  and grant us your salvation.

I will listen to what God the LORD
    will say;
  he promises peace to his people,
    his saints—
  but let them not return to folly.
Surely his salvation is near those
    who fear him,
  that his glory may dwell in our
    land.

Love and faithfulness meet
    together;
  righteousness and peace kiss
    each other.
Faithfulness springs forth from the
    earth,
  and righteousness looks down
    from heaven.
The LORD will indeed give what is
    good,
  and our land will yield its
    harvest.
Righteousness goes before him
  and prepares the way for his steps.

～

## Psalm 86
*A prayer of David.*

Hear, O LORD, and answer me,
　for I am poor and needy.
Guard my life, for I am devoted
　to you.
　You are my God; save your
　　servant
　who trusts in you.
Have mercy on me, O Lord,
　for I call to you all day long.
Bring joy to your servant,
　for to you, O Lord,
　I lift up my soul.

You are forgiving and good, O Lord,
　abounding in love to all who
　　call to you.
Hear my prayer, O LORD;
　listen to my cry for mercy.
In the day of my trouble I will
　　call to you,
　for you will answer me.

Among the gods there is none like
　you, O Lord;
　no deeds can compare with
　　yours.
All the nations you have made
　will come and worship before
　　you, O Lord;
　they will bring glory to your
　　name.
For you are great and do
　　marvellous deeds;
　you alone are God.

Teach me your way, O LORD,
　and I will walk in your truth;

give me an undivided heart,
　that I may fear your name.
I will praise you, O Lord my God,
　with all my heart;
　I will glorify your name for ever.
For great is your love towards me;
　you have delivered me from the
　　depths of the grave.

The arrogant are attacking me,
　O God;
　a band of ruthless men seeks
　　my life—
　men without regard for you.
But you, O Lord, are a
　　compassionate and gracious
　　God,
　slow to anger, abounding in
　　love and faithfulness.
Turn to me and have mercy on me;
　grant your strength to your
　　servant
　and save the son of your
　　maidservant.
Give me a sign of your goodness,
　that my enemies may see it and
　　be put to shame,
　for you, O LORD, have helped
　　me and comforted me.

∼

## Psalm 87
*Of the Sons of Korah. A psalm. A song.*

He has set his foundation on the
　　holy mountain;
　the LORD loves the gates of Zion
　more than all the dwellings of
　　Jacob.

Glorious things are said of you,
O city of God:                              *Selah*
"I will record Rahab and Babylon
among those who acknowledge
me—
Philistia too, and Tyre, along with
Cush—
and will say, 'This one was
born in Zion.' "

Indeed, of Zion it will be said,
"This one and that one were
born in her,
and the Most High himself will
establish her."
The LORD will write in the register
of the peoples:
"This one was born in Zion."
*Selah*
As they make music they will
sing,
"All my fountains are in you."

~

## Psalm 88

*A song. A psalm of the Sons of Korah.*
*For the director of music. According to*
mahalath leannoth. *A maskil of*
*Heman the Ezrahite.*

O LORD, the God who saves me,
day and night I cry out before
you.
May my prayer come before you;
turn your ear to my cry.

For my soul is full of trouble
and my life draws near the
grave.

I am counted among those who
go down to the pit;
I am like a man without
strength.
I am set apart with the dead,
like the slain who lie in the
grave,
whom you remember no more,
who are cut off from your care.

You have put me in the lowest
pit,
in the darkest depths.
Your wrath lies heavily upon me;
you have overwhelmed me with
all your waves.          *Selah*
You have taken from me my
closest friends
and have made me repulsive to
them.
I am confined and cannot escape;
my eyes are dim with grief.

I call to you, O LORD, every day;
I spread out my hands to you.
Do you show your wonders to the
dead?
Do those who are dead rise up
and praise you?          *Selah*
Is your love declared in the
grave,
your faithfulness in Destruction?
Are your wonders known in the
place of darkness,
or your righteous deeds in the
land of oblivion?

But I cry to you for help, O LORD;
in the morning my prayer
comes before you.

Why, O LORD, do you reject me
and hide your face from me?

From my youth I have been
afflicted and close to death;
I have suffered your terrors and
am in despair.
Your wrath has swept over me;
your terrors have destroyed me.
All day long they surround me
like a flood;
they have completely engulfed me.
You have taken my companions
and loved ones from me;
the darkness is my closest friend.

~

## Psalm 89

*A maskil of Ethan the Ezrahite.*

I will sing of the LORD's great love
for ever;
with my mouth I will make
your faithfulness known
through all generations.
I will declare that your love
stands firm for ever,
that you established your
faithfulness in heaven itself.

You said, "I have made a
covenant with my chosen
one,
I have sworn to David my
servant,
'I will establish your line for ever
and make your throne firm
through all generations.' "
*Selah*

The heavens praise your wonders,
O LORD,
your faithfulness too, in the
assembly of the holy ones.
For who in the skies above can
compare with the LORD?
Who is like the LORD among the
heavenly beings?
In the council of the holy ones
God is greatly feared;
he is more awesome than all
who surround him.
O LORD God Almighty, who is like
you?
You are mighty, O LORD, and your
faithfulness surrounds you.

You rule over the surging sea;
when its waves mount up, you
still them.
You crushed Rahab like one of the
slain;
with your strong arm you
scattered your enemies.
The heavens are yours, and yours
also the earth;
you founded the world and all
that is in it.
You created the north and the
south;
Tabor and Hermon sing for joy
at your name.
Your arm is endued with power;
your hand is strong, your right
hand exalted.

Righteousness and justice are the
foundation of your throne;
love and faithfulness go before
you.

Blessed are those who have
    learned to acclaim you,
  who walk in the light of your
    presence, O LORD.
They rejoice in your name all day
    long;
  they exult in your
    righteousness.
For you are their glory and
    strength,
  and by your favour you exalt
    our horn.
Indeed, our shield belongs to the
    LORD,
  our king to the Holy One of
    Israel.

Once you spoke in a vision,
  to your faithful people you
    said:
"I have bestowed strength on a
    warrior;
  I have exalted a young man
    from among the people.
I have found David my servant;
  with my sacred oil I have
    anointed him.
My hand will sustain him;
  surely my arm will strengthen
    him.
No enemy will subject him to
    tribute;
  no wicked man will oppress
    him.
I will crush his foes before him
  and strike down his
    adversaries.
My faithful love will be with him,
  and through my name his horn
    will be exalted.

I will set his hand over the sea,
  his right hand over the rivers.
He will call out to me, 'You are
    my Father,
  my God, the Rock my Saviour.'
I will also appoint him my firstborn,
  the most exalted of the kings of
    the earth.
I will maintain my love to him for
    ever,
  and my covenant with him will
    never fail.
I will establish his line for ever,
  his throne as long as the
    heavens endure.

"If his sons forsake my law
  and do not follow my statutes,
if they violate my decrees
  and fail to keep my commands,
I will punish their sin with the
    rod,
  their iniquity with flogging;
but I will not take my love from
    him,
  nor will I ever betray my
    faithfulness.
I will not violate my covenant
  or alter what my lips have
    uttered.
Once for all, I have sworn by my
    holiness—
  and I will not lie to David—
that his line will continue for ever
  and his throne endure before
    me like the sun;
it will be established for ever like
    the moon,
  the faithful witness in the sky."
                  *Selah*

But you have rejected, you have
    spurned,
        you have been very angry with
            your anointed one.
You have renounced the covenant
    with your servant
        and have defiled his crown in
            the dust.
You have broken through all his
    walls
        and reduced his strongholds to
            ruins.
All who pass by have plundered
    him;
        he has become the scorn of his
            neighbours.
You have exalted the right hand
    of his foes;
        you have made all his enemies
            rejoice.
You have turned back the edge of
    his sword
        and have not supported him in
            battle.
You have put an end to his
    splendour
        and cast his throne to the
            ground.
You have cut short the days of his
    youth;
        you have covered him with a
            mantle of shame.        *Selah*

How long, O LORD? Will you hide
    yourself for ever?
        How long will your wrath burn
            like fire?
Remember how fleeting is my life.
    For what futility you have
        created all men!

What man can live and not see
    death,
        or save himself from the power
            of the grave?        *Selah*
O Lord, where is your former
    great love,
        which in your faithfulness you
            swore to David?
Remember, Lord, how your
        servant has been mocked,
    how I bear in my heart the
        taunts of all the nations,
the taunts with which your
        enemies have mocked,
    O LORD,
        with which they have mocked
            every step of your anointed
                one.

Praise be to the LORD for ever!
    Amen and Amen.

# Book IV (Psalms 90–106)

## Psalm 90
*A prayer of Moses the man of God.*

Lord, you have been our
        dwelling-place
    throughout all generations.
Before the mountains were born
    or you brought forth the earth
        and the world,
        from everlasting to everlasting
            you are God.

You turn men back to dust,
    saying, "Return to dust, O sons
        of men."

For a thousand years in your sight
   are like a day that has just gone
      by,
   or like a watch in the night.
You sweep men away in the sleep
   of death;
   they are like the new grass of
      the morning—
though in the morning it springs
   up new,
   by evening it is dry and
      withered.

We are consumed by your anger
   and terrified by your
      indignation.
You have set our iniquities before
   you,
   our secret sins in the light of
      your presence.
All our days pass away under
   your wrath;
   we finish our years with a
      moan.
The length of our days is seventy
   years—
   or eighty, if we have the strength;
yet their span is but trouble and
   sorrow,
   for they quickly pass, and we
      fly away.

Who knows the power of your
   anger?
   For your wrath is as great as
      the fear that is due to you.
Teach us to number our days
   aright,
   that we may gain a heart of
      wisdom.

Relent, O LORD! How long will it
   be?
   Have compassion on your
      servants.
Satisfy us in the morning with
   your unfailing love,
   that we may sing for joy and be
      glad all our days.
Make us glad for as many days as
   you have afflicted us,
   for as many years as we have
      seen trouble.
May your deeds be shown to your
   servants,
   your splendour to their children.

May the favour of the Lord our
      God rest upon us;
   establish the work of our hands
      for us—
   yes, establish the work of our
      hands.

≈

# Psalm 91

He who dwells in the shelter of
      the Most High
   will rest in the shadow of the
      Almighty.
I will say of the LORD, "He is my
      refuge and my fortress,
   my God, in whom I trust."

Surely he will save you from the
   fowler's snare
   and from the deadly pestilence.
He will cover you with his
   feathers,

and under his wings you will
find refuge;
his faithfulness will be your
shield and rampart.
You will not fear the terror of
night,
nor the arrow that flies by
day,
nor the pestilence that stalks in
the darkness,
nor the plague that destroys at
midday.
A thousand may fall at your
side,
ten thousand at your right
hand,
but it will not come near you.
You will only observe with your
eyes
and see the punishment of the
wicked.

If you make the Most High your
dwelling—
even the Lord, who is my
refuge—
then no harm will befall you,
no disaster will come near your
tent.
For he will command his angels
concerning you
to guard you in all your ways;
they will lift you up in their
hands,
so that you will not strike your
foot against a stone.
You will tread upon the lion and
the cobra;
you will trample the great lion
and the serpent.

"Because he loves me," says the
Lord, "I will rescue him;
I will protect him, for he
acknowledges my name.
He will call upon me, and I will
answer him;
I will be with him in trouble,
I will deliver him and honour him.
With long life will I satisfy him
and show him my salvation."

∾

## Psalm 92
*A psalm. A song. For the Sabbath day.*

It is good to praise the Lord
and make music to your name,
O Most High,
to proclaim your love in the
morning
and your faithfulness at night,
to the music of the ten-stringed lyre
and the melody of the harp.

For you make me glad by your
deeds, O Lord;
I sing for joy at the work of
your hands.
How great are your works, O Lord,
how profound your thoughts!
The senseless man does not know,
fools do not understand,
that though the wicked spring up
like grass
and all evildoers flourish,
they will be for ever destroyed.

But you, O Lord, are exalted for
ever.

For surely your enemies, O LORD,
  surely your enemies will
    perish;
  all evildoers will be scattered.
You have exalted my horn like
    that of a wild ox;
  fine oils have been poured upon
    me.
My eyes have seen the defeat of
    my adversaries;
  my ears have heard the rout of
    my wicked foes.

The righteous will flourish like a
    palm tree,
  they will grow like a cedar of
    Lebanon;
planted in the house of the LORD,
  they will flourish in the courts
    of our God.
They will still bear fruit in old
    age,
  they will stay fresh and green,
proclaiming, "The LORD is upright;
  he is my Rock, and there is no
    wickedness in him."

∼

## Psalm 93

The LORD reigns, he is robed in
    majesty;
  the LORD is robed in majesty
  and is armed with strength.
The world is firmly established;
  it cannot be moved.
Your throne was established long
    ago;
  you are from all eternity.

The seas have lifted up, O LORD,
  the seas have lifted up their
    voice;
  the seas have lifted up their
    pounding waves.
Mightier than the thunder of the
    great waters,
  mightier than the breakers of
    the sea—
  the LORD on high is mighty.

Your statutes stand firm;
  holiness adorns your house
  for endless days, O LORD.

∼

## Psalm 94

O LORD, the God who avenges,
  O God who avenges, shine
    forth.
Rise up, O Judge of the earth;
  pay back to the proud what
    they deserve.
How long will the wicked,
    O LORD,
  how long will the wicked be
    jubilant?

They pour out arrogant words;
  all the evildoers are full of
    boasting.
They crush your people, O LORD;
  they oppress your inheritance.
They slay the widow and the
    alien;
  they murder the fatherless.
They say, "The LORD does not see;
  the God of Jacob pays no heed."

Take heed, you senseless ones
among the people;
you fools, when will you
become wise?
Does he who implanted the ear
not hear?
Does he who formed the eye
not see?
Does he who disciplines nations
not punish?
Does he who teaches man lack
knowledge?
The LORD knows the thoughts of
man;
he knows that they are futile.

Blessed is the man you discipline,
O LORD,
the man you teach from your
law;
you grant him relief from days of
trouble,
till a pit is dug for the wicked.
For the LORD will not reject his
people;
he will never forsake his
inheritance.
Judgment will again be founded
on righteousness,
and all the upright in heart will
follow it.

Who will rise up for me against
the wicked?
Who will take a stand for me
against evildoers?
Unless the LORD had given me
help,
I would soon have dwelt in the
silence of death.

When I said, "My foot is
slipping,"
your love, O LORD, supported
me.
When anxiety was great within
me,
your consolation brought joy to
my soul.

Can a corrupt throne be allied
with you—
one that brings on misery by its
decrees?
They band together against the
righteous
and condemn the innocent to
death.
But the LORD has become my
fortress,
and my God the rock in whom
I take refuge.
He will repay them for their
sins
and destroy them for their
wickedness;
the LORD our God will destroy
them.

⁓

## Psalm 95

Come, let us sing for joy to the
LORD;
let us shout aloud to the Rock
of our salvation.
Let us come before him with
thanksgiving
and extol him with music and
song.

For the LORD is the great God,
the great King above all gods.
In his hand are the depths of the
earth,
and the mountain peaks belong
to him.
The sea is his, for he made it,
and his hands formed the dry
land.

Come, let us bow down in
worship,
let us kneel before the LORD our
Maker;
for he is our God
and we are the people of his
pasture,
the flock under his care.

Today, if you hear his voice,
do not harden your hearts as
you did at Meribah,
as you did that day at Massah
in the desert,
where your fathers tested and
tried me,
though they had seen what I
did.
For forty years I was angry with
that generation;
I said, "They are a people
whose hearts go astray,
and they have not known my
ways."
So I declared on oath in my
anger,
"They shall never enter my
rest."

## Psalm 96

Sing to the LORD a new song;
sing to the LORD, all the earth.
Sing to the LORD, praise his
name;
proclaim his salvation day after
day.
Declare his glory among the
nations,
his marvellous deeds among all
peoples.

For great is the LORD and most
worthy of praise;
he is to be feared above all
gods.
For all the gods of the nations are
idols,
but the LORD made the heavens.
Splendour and majesty are before
him;
strength and glory are in his
sanctuary.

Ascribe to the LORD, O families of
nations,
ascribe to the LORD glory and
strength.
Ascribe to the LORD the glory due
to his name;
bring an offering and come into
his courts.
Worship the LORD in the
splendour of his holiness;
tremble before him, all the
earth.

Say among the nations, "The LORD
reigns."

The world is firmly established,
  it cannot be moved;
he will judge the peoples with
  equity.
Let the heavens rejoice, let the
  earth be glad;
  let the sea resound, and all that
    is in it;
  let the fields be jubilant, and
    everything in them.
Then all the trees of the forest will
  sing for joy;
  they will sing before the LORD,
    for he comes,
he comes to judge the earth.
He will judge the world in
  righteousness
  and the peoples in his truth.

∿

## Psalm 97

The LORD reigns, let the earth be
  glad;
  let the distant shores rejoice.

Clouds and thick darkness
  surround him;
  righteousness and justice are
    the foundation of his
    throne.
Fire goes before him
  and consumes his foes on every
    side.
His lightning lights up the world;
  the earth sees and trembles.
The mountains melt like wax
  before the LORD,
  before the Lord of all the earth.

The heavens proclaim his
  righteousness,
  and all the peoples see his
    glory.

All who worship images are put
  to shame,
  those who boast in idols—
  worship him, all you gods!

Zion hears and rejoices
  and the villages of Judah are
    glad
  because of your judgments,
    O LORD.
For you, O LORD, are the Most
  High over all the earth;
  you are exalted far above all
    gods.

Let those who love the LORD hate
  evil,
  for he guards the lives of his
    faithful ones
  and delivers them from the
    hand of the wicked.
Light is shed upon the righteous
  and joy on the upright in heart.
Rejoice in the LORD, you who are
  righteous,
  and praise his holy name.

## Psalm 98
*A psalm.*

Sing to the LORD a new song,
  for he has done marvellous
    things;

his right hand and his holy arm
   have worked salvation for him.
The LORD has made his salvation
   known
   and revealed his righteousness
     to the nations.
He has remembered his love
   and his faithfulness to the house
     of Israel;
all the ends of the earth have seen
   the salvation of our God.

Shout for joy to the LORD, all the
   earth,
   burst into jubilant song with
     music;
make music to the LORD with the
   harp,
   with the harp and the sound of
     singing,
with trumpets and the blast of the
   ram's horn—
   shout for joy before the LORD,
     the King.

Let the sea resound, and
   everything in it,
   the world, and all who live
     in it.
Let the rivers clap their hands,
   let the mountains sing together
     for joy;
let them sing before the LORD,
   for he comes to judge the earth.
He will judge the world in
   righteousness
   and the peoples with equity.

## Psalm 99

The LORD reigns,
   let the nations tremble;
he sits enthroned between the
     cherubim,
   let the earth shake.
Great is the LORD in Zion;
   he is exalted over all the
     nations.
Let them praise your great and
     awesome name—
   he is holy.

The King is mighty, he loves
     justice—
   you have established equity;
in Jacob you have done
   what is just and right.
Exalt the LORD our God
   and worship at his footstool;
   he is holy.

Moses and Aaron were among his
     priests,
   Samuel was among those who
     called on his name;
they called on the LORD
   and he answered them.
He spoke to them from the pillar
     of cloud;
   they kept his statutes and the
     decrees he gave them.

O LORD our God,
   you answered them;
you were to Israel a forgiving
     God,
   though you punished their
     misdeeds.

Exalt the LORD our God
and worship at his holy
mountain,
for the LORD our God is holy.

## Psalm 100
*A psalm. For giving thanks.*

Shout for joy to the LORD, all the
earth.
Worship the LORD with
gladness;
come before him with joyful
songs.
Know that the LORD is God.
It is he who made us, and we
are his;
we are his people, the sheep of
his pasture.

Enter his gates with thanksgiving
and his courts with praise;
give thanks to him and praise
his name.
For the LORD is good and his love
endures for ever;
his faithfulness continues
through all generations.

## Psalm 101
*Of David. A psalm.*

I will sing of your love and
justice;
to you, O LORD, I will sing
praise.

I will be careful to lead a
blameless life—
when will you come to me?

I will walk in my house
with blameless heart.
I will set before my eyes
no vile thing.

The deeds of faithless men I hate;
they shall not cling to me.
Men of perverse heart shall be far
from me;
I will have nothing to do with evil.

Whoever slanders his neighbour
in secret,
him will I put to silence;
whoever has haughty eyes and a
proud heart,
him will I not endure.

My eyes will be on the faithful in
the land,
that they may dwell with me;
he whose walk is blameless
will minister to me.

No-one who practises deceit
will dwell in my house;
no-one who speaks falsely
will stand in my presence.

Every morning I will put to
silence
all the wicked in the land;
I will cut off every evildoer
from the city of the LORD.

## Psalm 102

*A prayer of an afflicted man. When he is faint and pours out his lament before the LORD.*

Hear my prayer, O LORD;
  let my cry for help come to you.
Do not hide your face from me
  when I am in distress.
Turn your ear to me;
  when I call, answer me quickly.

For my days vanish like smoke;
  my bones burn like glowing
    embers.
My heart is blighted and withered
    like grass;
  I forget to eat my food.
Because of my loud groaning
  I am reduced to skin and bones.
I am like a desert owl,
  like an owl among the ruins.
I lie awake; I have become
  like a bird alone on a roof.
All day long my enemies taunt me;
  those who rail against me use
    my name as a curse.
For I eat ashes as my food
  and mingle my drink with tears
because of your great wrath,
  for you have taken me up and
    thrown me aside.
My days are like the evening
    shadow;
  I wither away like grass.

But you, O LORD, sit enthroned for
    ever;
  your renown endures through
    all generations.

You will arise and have
    compassion on Zion,
  for it is time to show favour to
    her;
  the appointed time has come.
For her stones are dear to your
    servants;
  her very dust moves them to
    pity.
The nations will fear the name of
    the LORD,
  all the kings of the earth will
    revere your glory.
For the LORD will rebuild Zion
  and appear in his glory.
He will respond to the prayer of
    the destitute;
  he will not despise their plea.

Let this be written for a future
    generation,
  that a people not yet created
    may praise the LORD:
"The LORD looked down from his
    sanctuary on high,
  from heaven he viewed the
    earth,
to hear the groans of the prisoners
  and release those condemned to
    death."
So the name of the LORD will be
    declared in Zion
  and his praise in Jerusalem
when the peoples and the
    kingdoms
  assemble to worship the LORD.

In the course of my life he broke
    my strength;
  he cut short my days.

So I said:
> "Do not take me away, O my
> God, in the midst of my
> days;
> your years go on through all
> generations.
In the beginning you laid the
> foundations of the earth,
> and the heavens are the work of
> your hands.
They will perish, but you remain;
> they will all wear out like a
> garment.
Like clothing you will change
> them
> and they will be discarded.
But you remain the same,
> and your years will never
> end.
The children of your servants will
> live in your presence;
> their descendants will be
> established before you."

~

# Psalm 103
*Of David.*

Praise the LORD, O my soul;
> all my inmost being, praise his
> holy name.
Praise the LORD, O my soul,
> and forget not all his benefits—
who forgives all your sins
> and heals all your diseases,
who redeems your life from the
> pit
> and crowns you with love and
> compassion,

who satisfies your desires with
> good things
> so that your youth is renewed
> like the eagle's.

The LORD works righteousness
> and justice for all the
> oppressed.

He made known his ways to
> Moses,
> his deeds to the people of Israel:
The LORD is compassionate and
> gracious,
> slow to anger, abounding in
> love.
He will not always accuse,
> nor will he harbour his anger
> for ever;
he does not treat us as our sins
> deserve
> or repay us according to our
> iniquities.
For as high as the heavens are
> above the earth,
> so great is his love for those
> who fear him;
as far as the east is from the west,
> so far has he removed our
> transgressions from us.
As a father has compassion on his
> children,
> so the LORD has compassion on
> those who fear him;
for he knows how we are formed,
> he remembers that we are dust.
As for man, his days are like
> grass,
> he flourishes like a flower of the
> field;

the wind blows over it and it is
    gone,
  and its place remembers it no
    more.
But from everlasting to everlasting
  the LORD's love is with those
    who fear him,
  and his righteousness with their
    children's children—
with those who keep his covenant
  and remember to obey his
    precepts.

The LORD has established his
    throne in heaven,
  and his kingdom rules over all.

Praise the LORD, you his angels,
  you mighty ones who do his
    bidding,
  who obey his word.
Praise the LORD, all his heavenly
    hosts,
  you his servants who do his
    will.
Praise the LORD, all his works
  everywhere in his dominion.

Praise the LORD, O my soul.

~

# Psalm 104

Praise the LORD, O my soul.

O LORD my God, you are very
    great;
  you are clothed with splendour
    and majesty.

He wraps himself in light as with
    a garment;
  he stretches out the heavens like
    a tent
  and lays the beams of his upper
    chambers on their waters.
He makes the clouds his chariot
  and rides on the wings of the
    wind.
He makes winds his messengers,
  flames of fire his servants.

He set the earth on its
    foundations;
  it can never be moved.
You covered it with the deep as
    with a garment;
  the waters stood above the
    mountains.
But at your rebuke the waters
    fled,
  at the sound of your thunder
    they took to flight;
they flowed over the mountains,
  they went down into the
    valleys,
  to the place you assigned for
    them.
You set a boundary they cannot
    cross;
  never again will they cover the
    earth.

He makes springs pour water into
    the ravines;
  it flows between the mountains.
They give water to all the beasts
    of the field;
  the wild donkeys quench their
    thirst.

The birds of the air nest by the
waters;
they sing among the branches.
He waters the mountains from his
upper chambers;
the earth is satisfied by the fruit
of his work.
He makes grass grow for the cattle,
and plants for man to
cultivate—
bringing forth food from the
earth:
wine that gladdens the heart of
man,
oil to make his face shine,
and bread that sustains his
heart.
The trees of the LORD are well
watered,
the cedars of Lebanon that he
planted.
There the birds make their nests;
the stork has its home in the
pine trees.
The high mountains belong to the
wild goats;
the crags are a refuge for the
conies.

The moon marks off the seasons,
and the sun knows when to go
down.
You bring darkness, it becomes
night,
and all the beasts of the forest
prowl.
The lions roar for their prey
and seek their food from God.
The sun rises, and they steal
away;

they return and lie down in
their dens.
Then man goes out to his work,
to his labour until evening.

How many are your works,
O LORD!
In wisdom you made them all;
the earth is full of your
creatures.
There is the sea, vast and spacious,
teeming with creatures beyond
number—
living things both large and
small.
There the ships go to and fro,
and the leviathan, which you
formed to frolic there.

These all look to you
to give them their food at the
proper time.
When you give it to them,
they gather it up;
when you open your hand,
they are satisfied with good
things.
When you hide your face,
they are terrified!
when you take away their breath,
they die and return to the dust.
When you send your Spirit,
they are created,
and you renew the face of the
earth.

May the glory of the LORD endure
for ever;
may the LORD rejoice in his
works—

he who looks at the earth, and it
    trembles,
  who touches the mountains,
    and they smoke.

I will sing to the LORD all my life;
  I will sing praise to my God as
    long as I live.
May my meditation be pleasing to
  him,
  as I rejoice in the LORD.
But may sinners vanish from the
  earth
  and the wicked be no more.

Praise the LORD, O my soul.

Praise the LORD.

∾

# Psalm 105

Give thanks to the LORD, call on
  his name;
  make known among the nations
    what he has done.
Sing to him, sing praise to him;
  tell of all his wonderful acts.
Glory in his holy name;
  let the hearts of those who seek
    the LORD rejoice.
Look to the LORD and his strength;
  seek his face always.

Remember the wonders he has done,
  his miracles, and the judgments
    he pronounced,
O descendants of Abraham his
  servant,

O sons of Jacob, his chosen
    ones.
He is the LORD our God;
  his judgments are in all the
    earth.

He remembers his covenant for
  ever,
  the word he commanded, for a
    thousand generations,
the covenant he made with
  Abraham,
  the oath he swore to Isaac.
He confirmed it to Jacob as a
  decree,
  to Israel as an everlasting
    covenant:
"To you I will give the land of
  Canaan
  as the portion you will inherit."

When they were but few in
  number,
  few indeed, and strangers in it,
they wandered from nation to
  nation,
  from one kingdom to another.
He allowed no-one to oppress
  them;
  for their sake he rebuked
    kings:
"Do not touch my anointed ones;
  do my prophets no harm."

He called down famine on the
  land
  and destroyed all their supplies
    of food;
and he sent a man before them—
  Joseph, sold as a slave.

They bruised his feet with
       shackles,
   his neck was put in irons,
till what he foretold came to pass,
   till the word of the LORD proved
       him true.
The king sent and released him,
   the ruler of peoples set him free.
He made him master of his
       household,
   ruler over all he possessed,
to instruct his princes as he
       pleased
   and teach his elders wisdom.

Then Israel entered Egypt;
   Jacob lived as an alien in the
       land of Ham.
The LORD made his people very
       fruitful;
   he made them too numerous for
       their foes,
whose hearts he turned to hate his
       people,
   to conspire against his servants.
He sent Moses his servant,
   and Aaron, whom he had chosen.
They performed his miraculous
       signs among them,
   his wonders in the land of
       Ham.
He sent darkness and made the
       land dark—
   for had they not rebelled
       against his words?
He turned their waters into blood,
   causing their fish to die.
Their land teemed with frogs,
   which went up into the
       bedrooms of their rulers.

He spoke, and there came swarms
       of flies,
   and gnats throughout their
       country.
He turned their rain into hail,
   with lightning throughout their
       land;
he struck down their vines and
       fig-trees
   and shattered the trees of their
       country.
He spoke, and the locusts came,
   grasshoppers without number;
they ate up every green thing in
       their land,
   ate up the produce of their
       soil.
Then he struck down all the
       firstborn in their land,
   the firstfruits of all their
       manhood.

He brought out Israel, laden with
       silver and gold,
   and from among their tribes no-
       one faltered.
Egypt was glad when they left,
   because dread of Israel had
       fallen on them.
He spread out a cloud as a
       covering,
   and a fire to give light at night.
They asked, and he brought them
       quail
   and satisfied them with the
       bread of heaven.
He opened the rock, and water
       gushed out;
   like a river it flowed in the
       desert.

For he remembered his holy
    promise
  given to his servant Abraham.
He brought out his people with
    rejoicing,
  his chosen ones with shouts of
    joy;
he gave them the lands of the
    nations,
  and they fell heir to what others
    had toiled for—
that they might keep his
    precepts
  and observe his laws.

Praise the LORD.

≈

## Psalm 106

Praise the LORD.

Give thanks to the LORD, for he is
    good;
  his love endures for ever.
Who can proclaim the mighty acts
    of the LORD
  or fully declare his praise?
Blessed are they who maintain
    justice,
  who constantly do what is
    right.
Remember me, O LORD, when you
    show favour to your
    people,
  come to my aid when you save
    them,

that I may enjoy the prosperity of
    your chosen ones,
  that I may share in the joy of
    your nation
  and join your inheritance in
    giving praise.

We have sinned, even as our
    fathers did;
  we have done wrong and acted
    wickedly.
When our fathers were in Egypt,
  they gave no thought to your
    miracles;
they did not remember your many
    kindnesses,
  and they rebelled by the sea,
    the Red Sea.
Yet he saved them for his name's
    sake,
  to make his mighty power
    known.
He rebuked the Red Sea, and it
    dried up;
  he led them through the depths
    as through a desert.
He saved them from the hand of
    the foe;
  from the hand of the enemy he
    redeemed them.
The waters covered their
    adversaries;
  not one of them survived.
Then they believed his promises
  and sang his praise.

But they soon forgot what he had
    done
  and did not wait for his
    counsel.

In the desert they gave in to their
craving;
  in the wasteland they put God
  to the test.
So he gave them what they asked
for,
  but sent a wasting disease upon
  them.

In the camp they grew envious of
Moses
  and of Aaron, who was
  consecrated to the LORD.
The earth opened up and
  swallowed Dathan;
  it buried the company of
  Abiram.
Fire blazed among their followers;
  a flame consumed the wicked.

At Horeb they made a calf
  and worshipped an idol cast
  from metal.
They exchanged their Glory
  for an image of a bull, which
  eats grass.
They forgot the God who saved
  them,
  who had done great things in
  Egypt,
miracles in the land of Ham
  and awesome deeds by the Red
  Sea.
So he said he would destroy
  them—
  had not Moses, his chosen
  one,
stood in the breach before him
  to keep his wrath from
  destroying them.

Then they despised the pleasant
land;
  they did not believe his promise.
They grumbled in their tents
  and did not obey the LORD.
So he swore to them with uplifted
hand
  that he would make them fall in
  the desert,
make their descendants fall among
  the nations
  and scatter them throughout the
  lands.

They yoked themselves to the Baal
of Peor
  and ate sacrifices offered to
  lifeless gods;
they provoked the LORD to anger
  by their wicked deeds,
  and a plague broke out among
  them.
But Phinehas stood up and
  intervened,
  and the plague was checked.
This was credited to him as
  righteousness
  for endless generations to come.

By the waters of Meribah they
  angered the LORD,
  and trouble came to Moses
  because of them;
for they rebelled against the Spirit
  of God,
  and rash words came from
  Moses' lips.

They did not destroy the peoples
  as the LORD had commanded them,

but they mingled with the nations
    and adopted their customs.
They worshipped their idols,
    which became a snare to them.
They sacrificed their sons
    and their daughters to demons.
They shed innocent blood,
    the blood of their sons and
        daughters,
whom they sacrificed to the idols
    of Canaan,
    and the land was desecrated by
        their blood.
They defiled themselves by what
    they did;
    by their deeds they prostituted
        themselves.

Therefore the LORD was angry
    with his people
    and abhorred his inheritance.
He handed them over to the
    nations,
    and their foes ruled over them.
Their enemies oppressed them
    and subjected them to their
        power.
Many times he delivered them,
    but they were bent on rebellion
    and they wasted away in their
        sin.

But he took note of their distress
    when he heard their cry;
for their sake he remembered his
    covenant
    and out of his great love he
        relented.
He caused them to be pitied
    by all who held them captive.

Save us, O LORD our God,
    and gather us from the nations,
that we may give thanks to your
        holy name
    and glory in your praise.

Praise be to the LORD, the God of
        Israel,
    from everlasting to everlasting.
Let all the people say, "Amen!"

Praise the LORD.

# Book V (Psalms 107–150)

## Psalm 107

Give thanks to the LORD, for he is
        good;
    his love endures for ever.
Let the redeemed of the LORD say
        this—
    those he redeemed from the
        hand of the foe,
those he gathered from the lands,
    from east and west, from north
        and south.

Some wandered in desert
        wastelands,
    finding no way to a city where
        they could settle.
They were hungry and thirsty,
    and their lives ebbed away.
Then they cried out to the LORD in
        their trouble,
    and he delivered them from
        their distress.
He led them by a straight way

to a city where they could
settle.
Let them give thanks to the LORD
for his unfailing love
and his wonderful deeds for
men,
for he satisfies the thirsty
and fills the hungry with good
things.

Some sat in darkness and the
deepest gloom,
prisoners suffering in iron
chains,
for they had rebelled against the
words of God
and despised the counsel of the
Most High.
So he subjected them to bitter
labour;
they stumbled, and there was
no-one to help.
Then they cried to the LORD in
their trouble,
and he saved them from their
distress.
He brought them out of darkness
and the deepest gloom
and broke away their chains.
Let them give thanks to the LORD
for his unfailing love
and his wonderful deeds for men,
for he breaks down gates of
bronze
and cuts through bars of iron.

Some became fools through their
rebellious ways
and suffered affliction because
of their iniquities.

They loathed all food
and drew near the gates of
death.
Then they cried to the LORD in
their trouble,
and he saved them from their
distress.
He sent forth his word and healed
them;
he rescued them from the
grave.
Let them give thanks to the LORD
for his unfailing love
and his wonderful deeds for
men.
Let them sacrifice thank-offerings
and tell of his works with songs
of joy.

Others went out on the sea in
ships;
they were merchants on the
mighty waters.
They saw the works of the LORD,
his wonderful deeds in the deep.
For he spoke and stirred up a
tempest
that lifted high the waves.
They mounted up to the heavens
and went down to the
depths;
in their peril their courage
melted away.
They reeled and staggered like
drunken men;
they were at their wits' end.
Then they cried out to the LORD in
their trouble,
and he brought them out of
their distress.

He stilled the storm to a whisper;
  the waves of the sea were
    hushed.
They were glad when it grew
    calm,
  and he guided them to their
    desired haven.
Let them give thanks to the LORD
    for his unfailing love
  and his wonderful deeds for
    men.
Let them exalt him in the
    assembly of the people
  and praise him in the council of
    the elders.

He turned rivers into a desert,
  flowing springs into thirsty
    ground,
and fruitful land into a salt waste,
  because of the wickedness of
    those who lived there.
He turned the desert into pools of
    water
  and the parched ground into
    flowing springs;
there he brought the hungry to
    live,
  and they founded a city where
    they could settle.
They sowed fields and planted
    vineyards
  that yielded a fruitful harvest;
he blessed them, and their
    numbers greatly increased,
  and he did not let their herds
    diminish.

Then their numbers decreased,
  and they were humbled

by oppression, calamity and
    sorrow;
he who pours contempt on nobles
  made them wander in a
    trackless waste.
But he lifted the needy out of
    their affliction
  and increased their families like
    flocks.
The upright see and rejoice,
  but all the wicked shut their
    mouths.

Whoever is wise, let him heed
    these things
  and consider the great love of
    the LORD.

∽

## Psalm 108
*A song. A psalm of David.*

My heart is steadfast, O God;
  I will sing and make music with
    all my soul.
Awake, harp and lyre!
  I will awaken the dawn.
I will praise you, O LORD, among
    the nations;
  I will sing of you among the
    peoples.
For great is your love, higher than
    the heavens;
  your faithfulness reaches to the
    skies.
Be exalted, O God, above the
    heavens,
  and let your glory be over all
    the earth.

Save us and help us with your
   right hand,
   that those you love may be
      delivered.
God has spoken from his
   sanctuary:
   "In triumph I will parcel out
      Shechem
   and measure off the Valley of
      Succoth.
Gilead is mine, Manasseh is mine;
   Ephraim is my helmet,
   Judah my sceptre.
Moab is my washbasin,
   upon Edom I toss my sandal;
   over Philistia I shout in
      triumph."

Who will bring me to the fortified
   city?
Who will lead me to Edom?
Is it not you, O God, you who
   have rejected us
   and no longer go out with our
      armies?
Give us aid against the enemy,
   for the help of man is
      worthless.
With God we shall gain the victory,
   and he will trample down our
      enemies.

～

# Psalm 109

*For the director of music. Of David.*
*A psalm.*

O God, whom I praise,
   do not remain silent,

for wicked and deceitful men
   have opened their mouths
      against me;
   they have spoken against me
      with lying tongues.
With words of hatred they
   surround me;
   they attack me without
      cause.
In return for my friendship they
   accuse me,
   but I am a man of prayer.
They repay me evil for good,
   and hatred for my friendship.

Appoint an evil man to oppose
   him;
   let an accuser stand at his right
      hand.
When he is tried, let him be found
   guilty,
   and may his prayers condemn
      him.
May his days be few;
   may another take his place of
      leadership.
May his children be fatherless
   and his wife a widow.
May his children be wandering
   beggars;
   may they be driven from their
      ruined homes.
May a creditor seize all he has;
   may strangers plunder the fruits
      of his labour.
May no-one extend kindness to
   him
   or take pity on his fatherless
      children.
May his descendants be cut off,

their names blotted out from
the next generation.
May the iniquity of his fathers be
remembered before the
Lord;
  may the sin of his mother never
  be blotted out.
May their sins always remain
before the Lord,
  that he may cut off the
  memory of them from the
  earth.

For he never thought of doing a
kindness,
  but hounded to death the
  poor
  and the needy and the broken-
  hearted.
He loved to pronounce a curse—
may it come on him;
he found no pleasure in blessing—
may it be far from him.
He wore cursing as his garment;
  it entered into his body like
  water,
  into his bones like oil.
May it be like a cloak wrapped
about him,
  like a belt tied for ever round
  him.
May this be the Lord's payment to
my accusers,
  to those who speak evil of me.

But you, O Sovereign Lord,
  deal well with me for your
  name's sake;
  out of the goodness of your
  love, deliver me.

For I am poor and needy,
  and my heart is wounded
  within me.
I fade away like an evening
shadow;
  I am shaken off like a locust.
My knees give way from fasting;
  my body is thin and gaunt.
I am an object of scorn to my
accusers;
  when they see me, they shake
  their heads.

Help me, O Lord my God;
  save me in accordance with
  your love.
Let them know that it is your
hand,
  that you, O Lord, have done it.
They may curse, but you will
bless;
  when they attack they will be
  put to shame,
  but your servant will rejoice.
My accusers will be clothed with
disgrace
  and wrapped in shame as in a
  cloak.

With my mouth I will greatly
extol the Lord;
  in the great throng I will praise
  him.
For he stands at the right hand of
the needy one,
  to save his life from those who
  condemn him.

≈

# Psalm 110

*Of David. A psalm.*

The LORD says to my Lord:
　"Sit at my right hand
until I make your enemies
　a footstool for your feet."

The LORD will extend your mighty
　　sceptre from Zion;
　you will rule in the midst of
　　your enemies.
Your troops will be willing
　on your day of battle.
Arrayed in holy majesty,
　from the womb of the dawn
　you will receive the dew of
　　your youth.

The LORD has sworn
　and will not change his mind:
"You are a priest for ever,
　in the order of Melchizedek."

The Lord is at your right hand;
　he will crush kings on the day
　　of his wrath.
He will judge nations, heaping up
　　the dead
　and crushing the rulers of the
　　whole earth.
He will drink from a brook beside
　　the way;
　therefore he will lift up his
　　head.

# Psalm 111

Praise the LORD.

I will extol the LORD with all my
　　heart
　in the council of the upright
　　and in the assembly.

Great are the works of the LORD;
　they are pondered by all who
　　delight in them.
Glorious and majestic are his
　　deeds,
　and his righteousness endures
　　for ever.
He has caused his wonders to be
　　remembered;
　the LORD is gracious and
　　compassionate.
He provides food for those who
　　fear him;
　he remembers his covenant for
　　ever.
He has shown his people the
　　power of his works,
　giving them the lands of other
　　nations.
The works of his hands are
　　faithful and just;
　all his precepts are trustworthy.
They are steadfast for ever and
　　ever,
　done in faithfulness and
　　uprightness.
He provided redemption for his
　　people;
　he ordained his covenant for
　　ever—
　holy and awesome is his name.

The fear of the LORD is the
    beginning of wisdom;
  all who follow his precepts have
    good understanding.
To him belongs eternal praise.

~

## Psalm 112

Praise the LORD.

Blessed is the man who fears the
    LORD,
  who finds great delight in his
    commands.

His children will be mighty in the
    land;
  the generation of the upright
    will be blessed.
Wealth and riches are in his
    house,
  and his righteousness endures
    for ever.
Even in darkness light dawns for
    the upright,
  for the gracious and
    compassionate and
    righteous man.
Good will come to him who is
    generous and lends freely,
  who conducts his affairs with
    justice.
Surely he will never be shaken;
  a righteous man will be
    remembered for ever.
He will have no fear of bad news;
  his heart is steadfast, trusting in
    the LORD.

His heart is secure, he will have
    no fear;
  in the end he will look in
    triumph on his foes.
He has scattered abroad his gifts
    to the poor,
  his righteousness endures for ever;
  his horn will be lifted high in
    honour.

The wicked man will see and be
    vexed,
  he will gnash his teeth and
    waste away;
  the longings of the wicked will
    come to nothing.

~

## Psalm 113

Praise the LORD.

Praise, O servants of the LORD,
  praise the name of the LORD.
Let the name of the LORD be praised,
  both now and for evermore.
From the rising of the sun to the
    place where it sets,
  the name of the LORD is to be
    praised.

The LORD is exalted over all the
    nations,
  his glory above the heavens.
Who is like the LORD our God,
  the One who sits enthroned on
    high,
who stoops down to look
  on the heavens and the earth?

He raises the poor from the dust
　　and lifts the needy from the ash
　　　　heap;
he seats them with princes,
　　with the princes of their people.
He settles the barren woman in
　　her home
　　as a happy mother of children.

Praise the LORD.

~

# Psalm 114

When Israel came out of Egypt,
　　the house of Jacob from a
　　　　people of foreign tongue,
Judah became God's sanctuary,
　　Israel his dominion.

The sea looked and fled,
　　the Jordan turned back;
the mountains skipped like rams,
　　the hills like lambs.

Why was it, O sea, that you fled,
　　O Jordan, that you turned
　　　　back,
you mountains, that you skipped
　　like rams,
　　you hills, like lambs?

Tremble, O earth, at the presence
　　of the Lord,
　　at the presence of the God of
　　　　Jacob,
who turned the rock into a pool,
　　the hard rock into springs of
　　　　water.

# Psalm 115

Not to us, O LORD, not to us
　　but to your name be the glory,
　　because of your love and
　　　　faithfulness.

Why do the nations say,
　　"Where is their God?"
Our God is in heaven;
　　he does whatever pleases him.
But their idols are silver and gold,
　　made by the hands of men.
They have mouths, but cannot
　　speak,
　　eyes, but they cannot see;
they have ears, but cannot hear,
　　noses, but they cannot smell;
they have hands, but cannot feel,
　　feet, but they cannot walk;
　　nor can they utter a sound with
　　　　their throats.
Those who make them will be like
　　them,
　　and so will all who trust in them.

O house of Israel, trust in the
　　LORD—
　　he is their help and shield.
O house of Aaron, trust in the
　　LORD—
　　he is their help and shield.
You who fear him, trust in the
　　LORD—
　　he is their help and shield.

The LORD remembers us and will
　　bless us:
　　He will bless the house of
　　　　Israel,

he will bless the house of
  Aaron,
he will bless those who fear the
  LORD—
  small and great alike.

May the LORD make you increase,
  both you and your children.
May you be blessed by the LORD,
  the Maker of heaven and earth.

The highest heavens belong to the
  LORD,
  but the earth he has given to man.
It is not the dead who praise the
  LORD,
  those who go down to silence;
it is we who extol the LORD,
  both now and for evermore.

Praise the LORD.

∼

## Psalm 116

I love the LORD, for he heard my
  voice;
  he heard my cry for mercy.
Because he turned his ear to me,
  I will call on him as long as I live.

The cords of death entangled me,
  the anguish of the grave came
    upon me;
  I was overcome by trouble and
    sorrow.
Then I called on the name of the
  LORD:
  "O LORD, save me!"

The LORD is gracious and
  righteous;
  our God is full of compassion.
The LORD protects the simple-
  hearted;
  when I was in great need, he
    saved me.

Be at rest once more, O my
  soul,
  for the LORD has been good to
    you.

For you, O LORD, have delivered
  my soul from death,
  my eyes from tears,
  my feet from stumbling,
that I may walk before the LORD
  in the land of the living.
I believed; therefore I said,
  "I am greatly afflicted."
And in my dismay I said,
  "All men are liars."

How can I repay the LORD
  for all his goodness to me?
I will lift up the cup of salvation
  and call on the name of the
    LORD.
I will fulfil my vows to the LORD
  in the presence of all his
    people.

Precious in the sight of the LORD
  is the death of his saints.
O LORD, truly I am your servant;
  I am your servant, the son of
    your maidservant;
  you have freed me from my
    chains.

I will sacrifice a thank-offering to
    you
  and call on the name of the
      LORD.
I will fulfil my vows to the LORD
  in the presence of all his
      people,
in the courts of the house of the
    LORD—
  in your midst, O Jerusalem.

Praise the LORD.

# Psalm 117

Praise the LORD, all you nations;
  extol him, all you peoples.
For great is his love towards us,
  and the faithfulness of the LORD
      endures for ever.

Praise the LORD.

# Psalm 118

Give thanks to the LORD, for he is
    good;
  his love endures for ever.

Let Israel say:
  "His love endures for ever."
Let the house of Aaron say:
  "His love endures for ever."
Let those who fear the LORD say:
  "His love endures for ever."

In my anguish I cried to the LORD,
  and he answered by setting me
      free.
The LORD is with me; I will not be
    afraid.
  What can man do to me?
The LORD is with me; he is my
    helper.
  I will look in triumph on my
      enemies.

It is better to take refuge in the
    LORD
  than to trust in man.
It is better to take refuge in the
    LORD
  than to trust in princes.

All the nations surrounded me,
  but in the name of the LORD I
      cut them off.
They surrounded me on every side,
  but in the name of the LORD I
      cut them off.
They swarmed around me like
    bees,
  but they died out as quickly as
      burning thorns;
  in the name of the LORD I cut
      them off.

I was pushed back and about to fall,
  but the LORD helped me.
The LORD is my strength and my
    song;
  he has become my salvation.

Shouts of joy and victory
  resound in the tents of the
      righteous:

"The LORD's right hand has done
    mighty things!
  The LORD's right hand is lifted
    high;
  the LORD's right hand has done
    mighty things!"

I will not die but live,
  and will proclaim what the
    LORD has done.
The LORD has chastened me
    severely,
  but he has not given me over to
    death.

Open for me the gates of
    righteousness;
  I will enter and give thanks to
    the LORD.
This is the gate of the LORD
  through which the righteous
    may enter.
I will give you thanks, for you
    answered me;
  you have become my salvation.

The stone the builders rejected
  has become the capstone;
the LORD has done this,
  and it is marvellous in our eyes.
This is the day the LORD has
    made;
  let us rejoice and be glad in it.

O LORD, save us;
  O LORD, grant us success.
Blessed is he who comes in the
    name of the LORD.
  From the house of the LORD we
    bless you.

The LORD is God,
  and he has made his light shine
    upon us.
With boughs in hand, join in the
    festal procession
  up to the horns of the altar.

You are my God, and I will give
    thanks;
  you are my God, and I will
    exalt you.

Give thanks to the LORD, for he is
    good;
  his love endures for ever.

~

# Psalm 119

א Aleph

Blessed are they whose ways are
    blameless,
  who walk according to the law
    of the LORD.
Blessed are they who keep his
    statutes
  and seek him with all their
    heart.
They do nothing wrong;
  they walk in his ways.
You have laid down precepts
  that are to be fully obeyed.
Oh, that my ways were steadfast
  in obeying your decrees!
Then I would not be put to
    shame
  when I consider all your
    commands.

I will praise you with an upright
heart
as I learn your righteous laws.
I will obey your decrees;
do not utterly forsake me.

ב Beth

How can a young man keep his
way pure?
By living according to your
word.
I seek you with all my heart;
do not let me stray from your
commands.
I have hidden your word in my
heart
that I might not sin against you.
Praise be to you, O LORD;
teach me your decrees.
With my lips I recount
all the laws that come from
your mouth.
I rejoice in following your statutes
as one rejoices in great riches.
I meditate on your precepts
and consider your ways.
I delight in your decrees;
I will not neglect your word.

ג Gimel

Do good to your servant, and I
will live;
I will obey your word.
Open my eyes that I may see
wonderful things in your law.
I am a stranger on earth;
do not hide your commands
from me.

My soul is consumed with longing
for your laws at all times.
You rebuke the arrogant, who are
cursed
and who stray from your
commands.
Remove from me scorn and
contempt,
for I keep your statutes.
Though rulers sit together and
slander me,
your servant will meditate on
your decrees.
Your statutes are my delight;
they are my counsellors.

ד Daleth

I am laid low in the dust;
preserve my life according to
your word.
I recounted my ways and you
answered me;
teach me your decrees.
Let me understand the teaching of
your precepts;
then I will meditate on your
wonders.
My soul is weary with sorrow;
strengthen me according to
your word.
Keep me from deceitful ways;
be gracious to me through your
law.
I have chosen the way of truth;
I have set my heart on your
laws.
I hold fast to your statutes,
O LORD;
do not let me be put to shame.

I run in the path of your
commands,
for you have set my heart free.

ה He

Teach me, O LORD, to follow your
decrees;
then I will keep them to the
end.
Give me understanding, and I will
keep your law
and obey it with all my heart.
Direct me in the path of your
commands,
for there I find delight.
Turn my heart towards your
statutes
and not towards selfish gain.
Turn my eyes away from
worthless things;
preserve my life according to
your word.
Fulfil your promise to your
servant,
so that you may be feared.
Take away the disgrace I dread,
for your laws are good.
How I long for your precepts!
Preserve my life in your
righteousness.

ו Waw

May your unfailing love come to
me, O LORD,
your salvation according to
your promise;
then I will answer the one who
taunts me,

for I trust in your word.
Do not snatch the word of truth
from my mouth,
for I have put my hope in your
laws.
I will always obey your law,
for ever and ever.
I will walk about in freedom,
for I have sought out your
precepts.
I will speak of your statutes
before kings
and will not be put to shame,
for I delight in your commands
because I love them.
I lift up my hands to your
commands, which I love,
and I meditate on your decrees.

ז Zayin

Remember your word to your
servant,
for you have given me hope.
My comfort in my suffering is
this:
Your promise preserves my life.
The arrogant mock me without
restraint,
but I do not turn from your
law.
I remember your ancient laws,
O LORD,
and I find comfort in them.
Indignation grips me because of
the wicked,
who have forsaken your law.
Your decrees are the theme of my
song
wherever I lodge.

In the night I remember your
name, O LORD,
and I will keep your law.
This has been my practice:
I obey your precepts.

ת Heth

You are my portion, O LORD;
I have promised to obey your
words.
I have sought your face with all
my heart;
be gracious to me according to
your promise.
I have considered my ways
and have turned my steps to
your statutes.
I will hasten and not delay
to obey your commands.
Though the wicked bind me with
ropes,
I will not forget your law.
At midnight I rise to give you
thanks
for your righteous laws.
I am a friend to all who fear you,
to all who follow your precepts.
The earth is filled with your love,
O LORD;
teach me your decrees.

ט Teth

Do good to your servant
according to your word,
O LORD.
Teach me knowledge and good
judgment,
for I believe in your commands.

Before I was afflicted I went
astray,
but now I obey your word.
You are good, and what you do is
good;
teach me your decrees.
Though the arrogant have
smeared me with lies,
I keep your precepts with all
my heart.
Their hearts are callous and
unfeeling,
but I delight in your law.
It was good for me to be
afflicted
so that I might learn your
decrees.
The law from your mouth is more
precious to me
than thousands of pieces of
silver and gold.

י Yodh

Your hands made me and formed
me;
give me understanding to learn
your commands.
May those who fear you rejoice
when they see me,
for I have put my hope in your
word.
I know, O LORD, that your laws
are righteous,
and in faithfulness you have
afflicted me.
May your unfailing love be my
comfort,
according to your promise to
your servant.

Let your compassion come to me
that I may live,
for your law is my delight.
May the arrogant be put to shame
for wronging me without
cause;
but I will meditate on your
precepts.
May those who fear you turn to
me,
those who understand your
statutes.
May my heart be blameless
towards your decrees,
that I may not be put to shame.

 כ   Kaph

My soul faints with longing for
your salvation,
but I have put my hope in your
word.
My eyes fail, looking for your
promise;
I say, "When will you comfort
me?"
Though I am like a wineskin in
the smoke,
I do not forget your decrees.
How long must your servant wait?
When will you punish my
persecutors?
The arrogant dig pitfalls for me,
contrary to your law.
All your commands are
trustworthy;
help me, for men persecute me
without cause.
They almost wiped me from the
earth,

but I have not forsaken your
precepts.
Preserve my life according to your
love,
and I will obey the statutes of
your mouth.

ל   Lamedh

Your word, O Lord, is eternal;
it stands firm in the heavens.
Your faithfulness continues
through all generations;
you established the earth, and it
endures.
Your laws endure to this day,
for all things serve you.
If your law had not been my
delight,
I would have perished in my
affliction.
I will never forget your precepts,
for by them you have preserved
my life.
Save me, for I am yours;
I have sought out your
precepts.
The wicked are waiting to destroy
me,
but I will ponder your statutes.
To all perfection I see a limit;
but your commands are
boundless.

מ   Mem

Oh, how I love your law!
I meditate on it all day long.
Your commands make me wiser
than my enemies,

for they are ever with me.
I have more insight than all my
teachers,
for I meditate on your statutes.
I have more understanding than
the elders,
for I obey your precepts.
I have kept my feet from every
evil path
so that I might obey your word.
I have not departed from your
laws,
for you yourself have taught
me.
How sweet are your words to my
taste,
sweeter than honey to my
mouth!
I gain understanding from your
precepts;
therefore I hate every wrong
path.

נ  Nun

Your word is a lamp to my feet
and a light for my path.
I have taken an oath and
confirmed it,
that I will follow your righteous
laws.
I have suffered much;
preserve my life, O LORD,
according to your word.
Accept, O LORD, the willing praise
of my mouth,
and teach me your laws.
Though I constantly take my life
in my hands,
I will not forget your law.

The wicked have set a snare for me,
but I have not strayed from
your precepts.
Your statutes are my heritage for
ever;
they are the joy of my heart.
My heart is set on keeping your
decrees
to the very end.

ס  Samekh

I hate double-minded men,
but I love your law.
You are my refuge and my shield;
I have put my hope in your word.
Away from me, you evildoers,
that I may keep the commands
of my God!
Sustain me according to your
promise, and I shall live;
do not let my hopes be dashed.
Uphold me, and I shall be
delivered;
I shall always have regard for
your decrees.
You reject all who stray from your
decrees,
for their deceitfulness is in vain.
All the wicked of the earth you
discard like dross;
therefore I love your statutes.
My flesh trembles in fear of you;
I stand in awe of your laws.

ע  Ayin

I have done what is righteous and
just;
do not leave me to my oppressors.

Ensure your servant's well-being;
  let not the arrogant oppress me.
My eyes fail, looking for your
    salvation,
  looking for your righteous
    promise.
Deal with your servant according
    to your love
  and teach me your decrees.
I am your servant; give me
    discernment
  that I may understand your
    statutes.
It is time for you to act, O LORD;
  your law is being broken.
Because I love your commands
  more than gold, more than pure
    gold,
and because I consider all your
    precepts right,
  I hate every wrong path.

**פ**   Pe

Your statutes are wonderful;
  therefore I obey them.
The unfolding of your words
    gives light;
  it gives understanding to the
    simple.
I open my mouth and pant,
  longing for your commands.
Turn to me and have mercy on me,
  as you always do to those who
    love your name.
Direct my footsteps according to
    your word;
  let no sin rule over me.
Redeem me from the oppression
    of men,

that I may obey your precepts.
Make your face shine upon your
    servant
  and teach me your decrees.
Streams of tears flow from my
    eyes,
  for your law is not obeyed.

**צ**   Tsadhe

Righteous are you, O LORD,
  and your laws are right.
The statutes you have laid down
    are righteous;
  they are fully trustworthy.
My zeal wears me out,
  for my enemies ignore your
    words.
Your promises have been
    thoroughly tested,
  and your servant loves them.
Though I am lowly and despised,
  I do not forget your precepts.
Your righteousness is everlasting
  and your law is true.
Trouble and distress have come
    upon me,
  but your commands are my
    delight.
Your statutes are for ever right;
  give me understanding that I
    may live.

**ק**   Qoph

I call with all my heart; answer
    me, O LORD,
  and I will obey your decrees.
I call out to you; save me
  and I will keep your statutes.

I rise before dawn and cry for
 help;
  I have put my hope in your
   word.
My eyes stay open through the
   watches of the night,
  that I may meditate on your
   promises.
Hear my voice in accordance with
   your love;
  preserve my life, O LORD,
   according to your laws.
Those who devise wicked schemes
   are near,
  but they are far from your
   law.
Yet you are near, O LORD,
  and all your commands are
   true.
Long ago I learned from your
   statutes
  that you established them to
   last for ever.

ר Resh

Look upon my suffering and
   deliver me,
  for I have not forgotten your
   law.
Defend my cause and redeem
   me;
  preserve my life according to
   your promise.
Salvation is far from the wicked,
  for they do not seek out your
   decrees.
Your compassion is great, O LORD;
  preserve my life according to
   your laws.

Many are the foes who persecute
   me,
  but I have not turned from your
   statutes.
I look on the faithless with
   loathing,
  for they do not obey your
   word.
See how I love your precepts;
  preserve my life, O LORD,
   according to your love.
All your words are true;
  all your righteous laws are
   eternal.

ש Sin and Shin

Rulers persecute me without
   cause,
  but my heart trembles at your
   word.
I rejoice in your promise
  like one who finds great
   spoil.
I hate and abhor falsehood
  but I love your law.
Seven times a day I praise you
  for your righteous laws.
Great peace have they who love
   your law,
  and nothing can make them
   stumble.
I wait for your salvation, O LORD,
  and I follow your commands.
I obey your statutes,
  for I love them greatly.
I obey your precepts and your
   statutes,
  for all my ways are known to
   you.

ת Taw

May my cry come before you, O
  LORD;
  give me understanding
    according to your word.
May my supplication come before
    you;
  deliver me according to your
    promise.
May my lips overflow with praise,
  for you teach me your decrees.
May my tongue sing of your word,
  for all your commands are
    righteous.
May your hand be ready to help
    me,
  for I have chosen your precepts.
I long for your salvation, O LORD,
  and your law is my delight.
Let me live that I may praise you,
  and may your laws sustain me.
I have strayed like a lost sheep.
  Seek your servant,
  for I have not forgotten your
    commands.

~

## Psalm 120

*A song of ascents.*

I call on the LORD in my distress,
  and he answers me.
Save me, O LORD, from lying lips
  and from deceitful tongues.

What will he do to you,
  and what more besides,
    O deceitful tongue?

He will punish you with a
    warrior's sharp arrows,
  with burning coals of the broom
    tree.

Woe to me that I dwell in Meshech,
  that I live among the tents of
    Kedar!
Too long have I lived
  among those who hate peace.
I am a man of peace;
  but when I speak, they are for
    war.

~

## Psalm 121

*A song of ascents.*

I lift up my eyes to the hills—
  where does my help come from?
My help comes from the LORD,
  the Maker of heaven and earth.

He will not let your foot slip—
  he who watches over you will
    not slumber;
indeed, he who watches over
    Israel
  will neither slumber nor sleep.

The LORD watches over you—
  the LORD is your shade at your
    right hand;
the sun will not harm you by day,
  nor the moon by night.

The LORD will keep you from all
    harm—
  he will watch over your life;

the LORD will watch over your
coming and going
both now and for evermore.

## Psalm 122

*A song of ascents. Of David.*

I rejoiced with those who said to
me,
"Let us go to the house of the
LORD."
Our feet are standing
in your gates, O Jerusalem.

Jerusalem is built like a city
that is closely compacted
together.
That is where the tribes go up,
the tribes of the LORD,
to praise the name of the LORD
according to the statute given to
Israel.
There the thrones for judgment
stand,
the thrones of the house of
David.

Pray for the peace of Jerusalem:
"May those who love you be
secure.
May there be peace within your
walls
and security within your
citadels."
For the sake of my brothers and
friends,
I will say, "Peace be within
you."

For the sake of the house of the
LORD our God,
I will seek your prosperity.

## Psalm 123

*A song of ascents.*

I lift up my eyes to you,
to you whose throne is in
heaven.
As the eyes of slaves look to the
hand of their master,
as the eyes of a maid look to
the hand of her mistress,
so our eyes look to the LORD our
God,
till he shows us his mercy.

Have mercy on us, O LORD, have
mercy on us,
for we have endured much
contempt.
We have endured much ridicule
from the proud,
much contempt from the
arrogant.

## Psalm 124

*A song of ascents. Of David.*

If the LORD had not been on our
side—
let Israel say—
if the LORD had not been on our
side
when men attacked us,

when their anger flared against us,
  they would have swallowed us
    alive;
the flood would have engulfed us,
  the torrent would have swept
    over us,
the raging waters
  would have swept us away.

Praise be to the LORD,
  who has not let us be torn by
    their teeth.
We have escaped like a bird
  out of the fowler's snare;
the snare has been broken,
  and we have escaped.
Our help is in the name of the
    LORD,
  the Maker of heaven and earth.

~

## Psalm 125
*A song of ascents.*

Those who trust in the LORD are
    like Mount Zion,
  which cannot be shaken but
    endures for ever.
As the mountains surround
    Jerusalem,
  so the LORD surrounds his people
both now and for evermore.

The sceptre of the wicked will not
    remain
  over the land allotted to the
    righteous,
for then the righteous might use
  their hands to do evil.

Do good, O LORD, to those who
    are good,
  to those who are upright in
    heart.
But those who turn to crooked ways
  the LORD will banish with the
    evildoers.

Peace be upon Israel.

~

## Psalm 126
*A song of ascents.*

When the LORD brought back the
    captives to Zion,
  we were like men who
    dreamed.
Our mouths were filled with
    laughter,
  our tongues with songs of joy.
Then it was said among the
    nations,
  "The LORD has done great things
    for them."
The LORD has done great things
    for us,
  and we are filled with joy.

Restore our fortunes, O LORD,
  like streams in the Negev.
Those who sow in tears
  will reap with songs of joy.
He who goes out weeping,
  carrying seed to sow,
will return with songs of joy,
  carrying sheaves with him.

~

## Psalm 127
*A song of ascents. Of Solomon.*

Unless the LORD builds the house,
  its builders labour in vain.
Unless the LORD watches over the
    city,
  the watchmen stand guard in
    vain.
In vain you rise early
  and stay up late,
toiling for food to eat—
  for he grants sleep to those he
    loves.

Sons are a heritage from the LORD,
  children a reward from him.
Like arrows in the hands of a
    warrior
  are sons born in one's youth.
Blessed is the man
  whose quiver is full of them.
They will not be put to shame
  when they contend with their
    enemies in the gate.

～

## Psalm 128
*A song of ascents.*

Blessed are all who fear the LORD,
  who walk in his ways.
You will eat the fruit of your
    labour;
  blessings and prosperity will be
    yours.
Your wife will be like a fruitful
    vine
  within your house;

your sons will be like olive shoots
  round your table.
Thus is the man blessed
  who fears the LORD.

May the LORD bless you from Zion
  all the days of your life;
may you see the prosperity of
    Jerusalem,
  and may you live to see your
    children's children.

Peace be upon Israel.

～

## Psalm 129
*A song of ascents.*

They have greatly oppressed me
    from my youth—
  let Israel say—
they have greatly oppressed me
    from my youth,
  but they have not gained the
    victory over me.
Ploughmen have ploughed my
    back
  and made their furrows long.
But the LORD is righteous;
  he has cut me free from the
    cords of the wicked.

May all who hate Zion
  be turned back in shame.
May they be like grass on the roof,
  which withers before it can
    grow;
with it the reaper cannot fill his
    hands,

nor the one who gathers fill his
  arms.
May those who pass by not say,
  "The blessing of the LORD be
    upon you;
  we bless you in the name of the
    LORD."

~

## Psalm 130
*A song of ascents.*

Out of the depths I cry to you,
  O LORD;
  O Lord, hear my voice.
Let your ears be attentive
  to my cry for mercy.

If you, O LORD, kept a record of sins,
  O Lord, who could stand?
But with you there is forgiveness;
  therefore you are feared.

I wait for the LORD, my soul waits,
  and in his word I put my hope.
My soul waits for the Lord
  more than watchmen wait for
    the morning,
  more than watchmen wait for
    the morning.

O Israel, put your hope in the LORD,
  for with the LORD is unfailing love
  and with him is full
    redemption.
He himself will redeem Israel
  from all their sins.

~

## Psalm 131
*A song of ascents. Of David.*

My heart is not proud, O LORD,
  my eyes are not haughty;
I do not concern myself with great
    matters
  or things too wonderful for me.
But I have stilled and quietened
    my soul;
  like a weaned child with its
    mother,
  like a weaned child is my soul
    within me.

O Israel, put your hope in the LORD
  both now and for evermore.

~

## Psalm 132
*A song of ascents.*

O LORD, remember David
  and all the hardships he endured.

He swore an oath to the LORD
  and made a vow to the Mighty
    One of Jacob:
"I will not enter my house
  or go to my bed—
I will allow no sleep to my eyes,
  no slumber to my eyelids,
till I find a place for the LORD,
  a dwelling for the Mighty One
    of Jacob."

We heard it in Ephrathah,
  we came upon it in the fields of
    Jaar:

"Let us go to his dwelling-place;
    let us worship at his footstool—
arise, O LORD, and come to your
        resting place,
    you and the ark of your might.
May your priests be clothed with
        righteousness;
    may your saints sing for joy."

For the sake of David your
        servant,
    do not reject your anointed
        one.

The LORD swore an oath to David,
    a sure oath that he will not
        revoke:
"One of your own descendants
    I will place on your throne—
if your sons keep my covenant
    and the statutes I teach them,
then their sons shall sit
    on your throne for ever and
        ever."

For the LORD has chosen Zion,
    he has desired it for his
        dwelling:
"This is my resting place for ever
        and ever;
    here I will sit enthroned, for I
        have desired it—
I will bless her with abundant
        provisions;
    her poor will I satisfy with
        food.
I will clothe her priests with
        salvation,
    and her saints shall ever sing
        for joy.

"Here I will make a horn grow for
        David
    and set up a lamp for my
        anointed one.
I will clothe his enemies with
        shame,
    but the crown on his head shall
        be resplendent."

∽

## Psalm 133
*A song of ascents. Of David.*

How good and pleasant it is
    when brothers live together in
        unity!
It is like precious oil poured on
        the head,
    running down on the beard,
running down on Aaron's beard,
    down upon the collar of his
        robes.
It is as if the dew of Hermon
    were falling on Mount Zion.
For there the LORD bestows his
        blessing,
    even life for evermore.

∽

## Psalm 134
*A song of ascents.*

Praise the LORD, all you servants
        of the LORD
    who minister by night in the
        house of the LORD.
Lift up your hands in the sanctuary
    and praise the LORD.

May the LORD, the Maker of
        heaven and earth,
    bless you from Zion.

~

## Psalm 135

Praise the LORD.

Praise the name of the LORD;
    praise him, you servants of the
        LORD,
you who minister in the house of
        the LORD,
    in the courts of the house of our
        God.

Praise the LORD, for the LORD is
        good;
    sing praise to his name, for that
        is pleasant.
For the LORD has chosen Jacob to
        be his own,
    Israel to be his treasured
        possession.

I know that the LORD is great,
    that our Lord is greater than all
        gods.
The LORD does whatever pleases
        him,
    in the heavens and on the
        earth,
    in the seas and all their depths.
He makes clouds rise from the
        ends of the earth;
    he sends lightning with the rain
    and brings out the wind from
        his storehouses.

He struck down the firstborn of
        Egypt,
    the firstborn of men and
        animals.
He sent his signs and wonders
        into your midst, O Egypt,
    against Pharaoh and all his
        servants.
He struck down many nations
    and killed mighty kings—
Sihon king of the Amorites,
    Og king of Bashan
    and all the kings of Canaan—
and he gave their land as an
        inheritance,
    an inheritance to his people
        Israel.

Your name, O LORD, endures for
        ever,
    your renown, O LORD, through
        all generations.
For the LORD will vindicate his
        people
    and have compassion on his
        servants.

The idols of the nations are silver
        and gold,
    made by the hands of men.
They have mouths, but cannot
        speak,
    eyes, but they cannot see;
they have ears, but cannot hear,
    nor is there breath in their
        mouths.
Those who make them will be like
        them,
    and so will all who trust in
        them.

O house of Israel, praise the LORD;
  O house of Aaron, praise the
  LORD;
O house of Levi, praise the LORD;
  you who fear him, praise the
  LORD.
Praise be to the LORD from Zion,
  to him who dwells in
  Jerusalem.

Praise the LORD.

~

# Psalm 136

Give thanks to the LORD, for he is
  good.
>   *His love endures for ever.*
Give thanks to the God of gods.
>   *His love endures for ever.*
Give thanks to the Lord of lords:
>   *His love endures for ever.*

to him who alone does great
  wonders,
>   *His love endures for ever.*
who by his understanding made
  the heavens,
>   *His love endures for ever.*
who spread out the earth upon
  the waters,
>   *His love endures for ever.*
who made the great lights—
>   *His love endures for ever.*
the sun to govern the day,
>   *His love endures for ever.*
the moon and stars to govern the
  night;
>   *His love endures for ever.*

to him who struck down the
  firstborn of Egypt
>   *His love endures for ever.*
and brought Israel out from
  among them
>   *His love endures for ever.*
with a mighty hand and
  outstretched arm;
>   *His love endures for ever.*

to him who divided the Red Sea
  asunder
>   *His love endures for ever.*
and brought Israel through the
  midst of it,
>   *His love endures for ever.*
but swept Pharaoh and his army
  into the Red Sea;
>   *His love endures for ever.*

to him who led his people
  through the desert,
>   *His love endures for ever.*
who struck down great kings,
>   *His love endures for ever.*
and killed mighty kings—
>   *His love endures for ever.*
Sihon king of the Amorites
>   *His love endures for ever.*
and Og king of Bashan—
>   *His love endures for ever.*
and gave their land as an
  inheritance,
>   *His love endures for ever.*
an inheritance to his servant Israel;
>   *His love endures for ever.*

to the One who remembered us in
  our low estate
>   *His love endures for ever.*

and freed us from our enemies,
> *His love endures for ever.*

and who gives food to every
creature.
> *His love endures for ever.*

Give thanks to the God of heaven.
> *His love endures for ever.*

~

## Psalm 137

By the rivers of Babylon we sat
and wept
when we remembered Zion.
There on the poplars
we hung our harps,
for there our captors asked us for
songs,
our tormentors demanded songs
of joy;
they said, "Sing us one of the
songs of Zion!"

How can we sing the songs of the
LORD
while in a foreign land?
If I forget you, O Jerusalem,
may my right hand forget its
skill.
May my tongue cling to the roof
of my mouth
if I do not remember you,
if I do not consider Jerusalem
my highest joy.

Remember, O LORD, what the
Edomites did
on the day Jerusalem fell.

"Tear it down," they cried,
"tear it down to its
foundations!"

O Daughter of Babylon, doomed
to destruction,
happy is he who repays you
for what you have done to us—
he who seizes your infants
and dashes them against the
rocks.

~

## Psalm 138
*Of David.*

I will praise you, O LORD, with all
my heart;
before the "gods" I will sing
your praise.
I will bow down towards your
holy temple
and will praise your name
for your love and your
faithfulness,
for you have exalted above all
things
your name and your word.
When I called, you answered me;
you made me bold and stout-
hearted.

May all the kings of the earth
praise you, O LORD,
when they hear the words of
your mouth.
May they sing of the ways of the
LORD,
for the glory of the LORD is great.

Though the LORD is on high, he
looks upon the lowly,
but the proud he knows from
afar.
Though I walk in the midst of
trouble,
you preserve my life;
you stretch out your hand against
the anger of my foes,
with your right hand you save
me.
The LORD will fulfil ˌhis purposeˌ
for me;
your love, O LORD, endures for
ever—
do not abandon the works of
your hands.

≈

## Psalm 139

*For the director of music. Of David.*
*A psalm.*

O LORD, you have searched me
and you know me.
You know when I sit and when I
rise;
you perceive my thoughts from
afar.
You discern my going out and my
lying down;
you are familiar with all my
ways.
Before a word is on my tongue
you know it completely,
O LORD.

You hem me in—behind and
before;

you have laid your hand upon
me.
Such knowledge is too wonderful
for me,
too lofty for me to attain.

Where can I go from your Spirit?
Where can I flee from your
presence?
If I go up to the heavens, you are
there;
if I make my bed in the depths,
you are there.
If I rise on the wings of the dawn,
if I settle on the far side of the
sea,
even there your hand will guide
me,
your right hand will hold me
fast.

If I say, "Surely the darkness will
hide me
and the light become night
around me,"
even the darkness will not be dark
to you;
the night will shine like the
day,
for darkness is as light to you.

For you created my inmost being;
you knit me together in my
mother's womb.
I praise you because I am fearfully
and wonderfully made;
your works are wonderful,
I know that full well.
My frame was not hidden from
you

when I was made in the secret
place.
When I was woven together in the
depths of the earth,
your eyes saw my unformed
body.
All the days ordained for me
were written in your book
before one of them came to be.

How precious to me are your
thoughts, O God!
How vast is the sum of
them!
Were I to count them,
they would outnumber the
grains of sand.
When I awake,
I am still with you.

If only you would slay the
wicked, O God!
Away from me, you
bloodthirsty men!
They speak of you with evil
intent;
your adversaries misuse your
name.
Do I not hate those who hate you,
O LORD,
and abhor those who rise up
against you?
I have nothing but hatred for
them;
I count them my enemies.

Search me, O God, and know my
heart;
test me and know my anxious
thoughts.

See if there is any offensive way
in me,
and lead me in the way
everlasting.

～

## Psalm 140
*For the director of music. A psalm of
David.*

Rescue me, O LORD, from evil
men;
protect me from men of
violence,
who devise evil plans in their
hearts
and stir up war every day.
They make their tongues as sharp
as a serpent's;
the poison of vipers is on their
lips.                              *Selah*

Keep me, O LORD, from the hands
of the wicked;
protect me from men of violence
who plan to trip my feet.
Proud men have hidden a snare
for me;
they have spread out the cords
of their net
and have set traps for me along
my path.                        *Selah*

O LORD, I say to you, "You are my
God."
Hear, O LORD, my cry for
mercy.
O Sovereign LORD, my strong
deliverer,

who shields my head in the day
of battle—
do not grant the wicked their
desires, O LORD;
  do not let their plans succeed,
  or they will become proud. *Selah*

Let the heads of those who
surround me
be covered with the trouble
their lips have caused.
Let burning coals fall upon them;
  may they be thrown into the
  fire,
  into miry pits, never to rise.
Let slanderers not be established
in the land;
  may disaster hunt down men of
  violence.

I know that the LORD secures
justice for the poor
and upholds the cause of the
needy.
Surely the righteous will praise
your name
and the upright will live before
you.

~

## Psalm 141
*A psalm of David.*

O LORD, I call to you; come
quickly to me.
  Hear my voice when I call to
  you.
May my prayer be set before you
like incense;

may the lifting up of my hands
be like the evening
sacrifice.

Set a guard over my mouth,
O LORD;
  keep watch over the door of my
  lips.
Let not my heart be drawn to
what is evil,
  to take part in wicked deeds
with men who are evildoers;
  let me not eat of their
  delicacies.

Let a righteous man strike me—it
is a kindness;
  let him rebuke me—it is oil on
  my head.
  My head will not refuse it.

Yet my prayer is ever against the
deeds of evildoers;
  their rulers will be thrown
  down from the cliffs,
  and the wicked will learn that
  my words were well
  spoken.
⌊They will say,⌋ "As one ploughs
and breaks up the earth,
  so our bones have been
  scattered at the mouth of
  the grave."

But my eyes are fixed on you,
O Sovereign LORD;
  in you I take refuge—do not
  give me over to death.
Keep me from the snares they
have laid for me,

from the traps set by evildoers.
Let the wicked fall into their own
nets,
while I pass by in safety.

~

## Psalm 142
*A maskil of David. When he was in the cave. A prayer.*

I cry aloud to the LORD;
I lift up my voice to the LORD
for mercy.
I pour out my complaint before
him;
before him I tell my trouble.

When my spirit grows faint
within me,
it is you who know my way.
In the path where I walk
men have hidden a snare for
me.
Look to my right and see;
no-one is concerned for me.
I have no refuge;
no-one cares for my life.

I cry to you, O LORD;
I say, "You are my refuge,
my portion in the land of the
living."
Listen to my cry,
for I am in desperate need;
rescue me from those who pursue
me,
for they are too strong for me.
Set me free from my prison,
that I may praise your name.

Then the righteous will gather
about me
because of your goodness to
me.

~

## Psalm 143
*A psalm of David.*

O LORD, hear my prayer,
listen to my cry for mercy;
in your faithfulness and
righteousness
come to my relief.
Do not bring your servant into
judgment,
for no-one living is righteous
before you.

The enemy pursues me,
he crushes me to the ground;
he makes me dwell in darkness
like those long dead.
So my spirit grows faint within me;
my heart within me is dismayed.

I remember the days of long ago;
I meditate on all your works
and consider what your hands
have done.
I spread out my hands to you;
my soul thirsts for you like a
parched land.          *Selah*

Answer me quickly, O LORD;
my spirit fails.
Do not hide your face from me
or I will be like those who go
down to the pit.

Let the morning bring me word of
　　your unfailing love,
　　for I have put my trust in you.
Show me the way I should go,
　　for to you I lift up my soul.
Rescue me from my enemies,
　　O LORD,
　　for I hide myself in you.
Teach me to do your will,
　　for you are my God;
may your good Spirit
　　lead me on level ground.

For your name's sake, O LORD,
　　preserve my life;
　　in your righteousness, bring me
　　out of trouble.
In your unfailing love, silence my
　　enemies;
　　destroy all my foes,
　　for I am your servant.

≈

## Psalm 144
*Of David.*

Praise be to the LORD my Rock,
　　who trains my hands for war,
　　my fingers for battle.
He is my loving God and my
　　fortress,
　　my stronghold and my
　　deliverer,
my shield, in whom I take refuge,
　　who subdues peoples under
　　me.

O LORD, what is man that you
　　care for him,

the son of man that you think
　　of him?
Man is like a breath;
　　his days are like a fleeting
　　shadow.

Part your heavens, O LORD, and
　　come down;
　　touch the mountains, so that
　　they smoke.
Send forth lightning and scatter
　　ˌthe enemiesˌ;
　　shoot your arrows and rout them.
Reach down your hand from on
　　high;
　　deliver me and rescue me
from the mighty waters,
　　from the hands of foreigners
whose mouths are full of lies,
　　whose right hands are deceitful.

I will sing a new song to you,
　　O God;
　　on the ten-stringed lyre I will
　　make music to you,
to the One who gives victory to
　　kings,
　　who delivers his servant David
　　from the deadly sword.

Deliver me and rescue me
　　from the hands of foreigners
whose mouths are full of lies,
　　whose right hands are deceitful.

Then our sons in their youth
　　will be like well-nurtured
　　plants,
and our daughters will be like
　　pillars

carved to adorn a palace.
Our barns will be filled
  with every kind of provision.
Our sheep will increase by
    thousands,
    by tens of thousands in our
      fields;
    our oxen will draw heavy
      loads.
There will be no breaching of
    walls,
  no going into captivity,
  no cry of distress in our streets.

Blessed are the people of whom
    this is true;
  blessed are the people whose
    God is the LORD.

~

## Psalm 145
*A psalm of praise. Of David.*

I will exalt you, my God the
    King;
  I will praise your name for ever
    and ever.
Every day I will praise you
  and extol your name for ever
    and ever.

Great is the LORD and most
    worthy of praise;
  his greatness no-one can
    fathom.
One generation will commend
    your works to another;
  they will tell of your mighty
    acts.

They will speak of the glorious
    splendour of your majesty,
  and I will meditate on your
    wonderful works.
They will tell of the power of
    your awesome works,
  and I will proclaim your great
    deeds.
They will celebrate your abundant
    goodness
  and joyfully sing of your
    righteousness.

The LORD is gracious and
    compassionate,
  slow to anger and rich in love.
The LORD is good to all;
  he has compassion on all he has
    made.
All you have made will praise
    you, O LORD;
  your saints will extol you.
They will tell of the glory of your
    kingdom
  and speak of your might,
so that all men may know of your
    mighty acts
  and the glorious splendour of
    your kingdom.
Your kingdom is an everlasting
    kingdom,
  and your dominion endures
    through all generations.

The LORD is faithful to all his
    promises
  and loving towards all he has
    made.
The LORD upholds all those who
    fall

and lifts up all who are bowed
down.
The eyes of all look to you,
and you give them their food at
the proper time.
You open your hand
and satisfy the desires of every
living thing.

The LORD is righteous in all his ways
and loving towards all he has
made.
The LORD is near to all who call
on him,
to all who call on him in truth.
He fulfils the desires of those who
fear him;
he hears their cry and saves them.
The LORD watches over all who
love him,
but all the wicked he will
destroy.

My mouth will speak in praise of
the LORD.
Let every creature praise his
holy name
for ever and ever.

∽

## Psalm 146

Praise the LORD.

Praise the LORD, O my soul.
I will praise the LORD all my
life;
I will sing praise to my God as
long as I live.

Do not put your trust in princes,
in mortal men, who cannot
save.
When their spirit departs, they
return to the ground;
on that very day their plans
come to nothing.

Blessed is he whose help is the
God of Jacob,
whose hope is in the LORD his
God,
the Maker of heaven and earth,
the sea, and everything in
them—
the LORD, who remains faithful
for ever.
He upholds the cause of the
oppressed
and gives food to the hungry.
The LORD sets prisoners free,
the LORD gives sight to the
blind,
the LORD lifts up those who are
bowed down,
the LORD loves the righteous.
The LORD watches over the alien
and sustains the fatherless and
the widow,
but he frustrates the ways of the
wicked.

The LORD reigns for ever,
your God, O Zion, for all
generations.

Praise the LORD.

∽

# Psalm 147

Praise the LORD.

How good it is to sing praises to
our God,
how pleasant and fitting to
praise him!

The LORD builds up Jerusalem;
he gathers the exiles of Israel.
He heals the broken-hearted
and binds up their wounds.

He determines the number of the
stars
and calls them each by name.
Great is our Lord and mighty in
power;
his understanding has no limit.
The LORD sustains the humble
but casts the wicked to the
ground.

Sing to the LORD with
thanksgiving;
make music to our God on the
harp.
He covers the sky with clouds;
he supplies the earth with rain
and makes grass grow on the
hills.
He provides food for the cattle
and for the young ravens when
they call.

His pleasure is not in the strength
of the horse,
nor his delight in the legs of a
man;

the LORD delights in those who
fear him,
who put their hope in his
unfailing love.

Extol the LORD, O Jerusalem;
praise your God, O Zion,
for he strengthens the bars of your
gates
and blesses your people within
you.
He grants peace to your borders
and satisfies you with the finest
of wheat.

He sends his command to the
earth;
his word runs swiftly.
He spreads the snow like wool
and scatters the frost like
ashes.
He hurls down hail like pebbles.
Who can withstand his icy
blast?
He sends his word and melts
them;
he stirs up his breezes, and the
waters flow.

He has revealed his word to
Jacob,
his laws and decrees to Israel.
He has done this for no other
nation;
they do not know his laws.

Praise the LORD.

❧

# Psalm 148

Praise the LORD.

Praise the LORD from the heavens,
  praise him in the heights above.
Praise him, all his angels,
  praise him, all his heavenly
    hosts.
Praise him, sun and moon,
  praise him, all you shining
    stars.
Praise him, you highest heavens
  and you waters above the skies.
Let them praise the name of the
    LORD,
  for he commanded and they
    were created.
He set them in place for ever and
    ever;
  he gave a decree that will never
    pass away.

Praise the LORD from the earth,
  you great sea creatures and all
    ocean depths,
lightning and hail, snow and
    clouds,
  stormy winds that do his
    bidding,
you mountains and all hills,
  fruit trees and all cedars,
wild animals and all cattle,
  small creatures and flying
    birds,
kings of the earth and all nations,
  you princes and all rulers on
    earth,
young men and maidens,
  old men and children.

Let them praise the name of the
    LORD,
  for his name alone is exalted;
  his splendour is above the earth
    and the heavens.
He has raised up for his people a
    horn,
  the praise of all his saints,
  of Israel, the people close to his
    heart.

Praise the LORD.

≈

# Psalm 149

Praise the LORD.

Sing to the LORD a new song,
  his praise in the assembly of the
    saints.

Let Israel rejoice in their Maker;
  let the people of Zion be glad in
    their King.
Let them praise his name with
    dancing
  and make music to him with
    tambourine and harp.
For the LORD takes delight in his
    people;
  he crowns the humble with
    salvation.
Let the saints rejoice in this honour
  and sing for joy on their beds.

May the praise of God be in their
    mouths
  and a double-edged sword in
    their hands,

to inflict vengeance on the nations
   and punishment on the peoples,
to bind their kings with fetters,
   their nobles with shackles of iron,
to carry out the sentence written
     against them.
   This is the glory of all his
     saints.

Praise the LORD.

## Psalm 150

Praise the LORD.

Praise God in his sanctuary;
   praise him in his mighty
     heavens.

Praise him for his acts of power;
   praise him for his surpassing
     greatness.
Praise him with the sounding of
     the trumpet,
   praise him with the harp and
     lyre,
praise him with tambourine and
     dancing,
   praise him with the strings and
     flute,
praise him with the clash of
     cymbals,
   praise him with resounding
     cymbals.

Let everything that has breath
     praise the LORD.

Praise the LORD.